Praise for A HAWAIIAN LIFE VOLUME 2

"This book is a 'must read' for anyone who loves Hawai`i! 'Uncle George K' magically weaves wit and wisdom into these stories and illustrations about growing up and living on an island in the middle of the sea. An unforgettable authentic Hawai`i memoir!"
— Joanne and Larry Laird, Co-Directors
Read Aloud America

"Aloha speaks through George's words."
— Wayne Moniz, Maui Born Playwright, Poet,
Author

"George Kahumoku's Hawaiian heart plus an endless supply of curiosity, humor and humility have produced a new book of stories to match his Grammy-winning musical accomplishments. As an artist, teacher, friend and neighbor, whatever he does, wherever he travels, he is the embodiment of aloha."
— Rick Chatenever. The Maui News

"A heart-warming treasure of memories from years gone by that recounts the experiences of Hawaiian youth in a way that reveals the true meaning of the Hawaiian Culture. A beautiful rendition and recollection of true life experiences of a Hawaiian growing up in the islands during a period of change and challenge."
— Mililani Trask, Hawaiian Movement Leader

"George Kahumoku exemplifies the successful fusion of contemporary and traditional Hawaiian culture – and the fusion of Hawaiian culture past and present with the culture of modern mainstream America"
—John Berger, Honolulu Star-Advertiser

"George has done it again. His 'sequel' is just as compelling as his first book in describing many of his experiences related to the Hawai'i of old. His books have become an anecdotal history of an era long gone."
—Andrew Kutsunai, Hawai'i Educator

"Colorful stories of how George's gifts of music and commitments to Hawaiian culture were influenced."
—Clyde M. Sakamoto, Chancellor, UH Maui College (Retired)

"George Kahumoku is a true Hawaiian Renaissance Man, an educator, farmer, great Slack Key guitarist, composer, song interpreter, sculptor, and more. His second book of life stories gives many wonderful insights for the inspirations for his songs, his playing, and shows his soulfulness for Hawai'i and humanity (and flora and fauna). His music has been a great inspiration to me since I first heard him in 1986."
—George Winston

Also by George Kahumoku, Jr.

A HAWAIIAN LIFE (VOLUME ONE)

George Kahumoku, Jr.

# A
# Hawaiian
# Life
## Volume Two

George Kahumoku, Jr.
As told to Paul Konwiser
Forward by Kathy Collins
Illustrated by George Kahumoku, Jr.

Kealia Press
Lahaina, Hawai'i

Cover photo by Dusty Foster
Illustrated by George Kahumoku, Jr.

Library of Congress Catalog Number
ISBN 978-0-9972068-0-7


Published by
Kealia Press
P.O. Box 12804
Lahaina, HI 96761

Printed in the United States of America

For my parents, my grandparents, my children, and my grandchildren.

--G.K.

George Kahumoku, Jr.

# Contents

**Da Stories**

**Small Kid Time**

**All Grown-up**

**Da Show**

**Recognition for George's Music**

# Foreword

The first time I saw George Kahumoku, Jr. in live performance, he was enthralling an audience of six or seven hundred at a Honolulu storytelling festival. Previously, all I knew of George was that he was a master of Hawaiian slack key guitar. That night at the Talk Story Festival, I learned that slack key is just one of the many facets of this multitalented gentleman who has been appropriately dubbed a "Hawaiian Renaissance Man."

Not only is George a gifted musician and songwriter, teller of tales and a contemporary cultural historian, he is an artist, a farmer, a fisherman, an educator and mentor. And unlike the proverbial "Jack of all trades, master of none," he actually excels in all that he undertakes.

As a storyteller and writer, I deeply appreciate and admire his ability to weave colorful, compelling narratives from the fabric of his remarkable life. When George tells a story, whether in a packed auditorium, a private conversation with a friend, or the pages of a book, he never fails to captivate with his delightful sense of humor and down-to-earth wisdom.

Most impressive of all, even with his myriad achievements and worldwide fame, he remains a genuinely humble, generous soul. Through these stories, George Kahumoku, Jr. truly exemplifies the aloha spirit.

*—Kathy Collins, Maui actress/storyteller*

# Introduction

I first met George Kahumoku Jr. at a concert at UCLA almost 20 years ago. With that meeting my life changed forever. George is like a whirlwind, and if you get too close to him you get pulled in. That has happened to me and many others. And it's been wonderful!

George is well known as Hawai'i's Renaissance man. He's a Grammy Award winning artist famed for his slack key guitar music. He's a teacher, an author, and an artist. He drew all of the illustrations for this book, in fact. More than anything, he's a farmer with deep roots in the land.

As anyone who's attended one of his concerts can tell you, George is also a master story teller. I've seen him engage audiences around the country with his wonderful tales. Our first book of stories, "A Hawaiian Life," is now in its fourth printing. Many copies have been distributed to schools here in Hawai'i, and those are the readers George likes best. He always hopes to inspire kids from a background similar to his.

As much as George loves to talk story, once he's off the stage it's not so easy to get him to sit down and record his tales. George is just about the busiest human on the planet. Besides farming and teaching, he plays gigs all over and is available to anyone who needs him. When we started work on the first book, I realized how difficult it was going to be to get enough time with him. I actually moved into his house in Lahaina for a week thinking that we'd get lots of stories written down. The day I arrived, George got a call from George Winston asking him to come to Honolulu for a recording session, and I ended up in his house by myself! When he got back at the end of the week he invited me to go to Hilo with him for a slack key festival. I had a wonderful time there, but I had to go back to the mainland with little to show for our time together. It turned out that the only way I could get quality time with him was to accompany him on tours, when he was away from his students, his goats, his ducks, his pigs and his taro.

I have found that George's stories vary considerably with each telling. Sometimes I'll hear a story that I've heard before, but this time there will be more details, many of which are especially poignant or funny. Some of his tales seem so wild that I've thought that he had to be exaggerating. Then I'll talk to someone else who was actually there, and find out that the true story is even wackier than George's description.

With this group of stories you'll hear about how it was for George growing up Hawaiian on islands that are quickly changing in character and culture. You'll meet "Kung Fu Tutu,"

George's tough-as-nails grandmother. You'll learn how George and his family got their education and survived tough times. And when George heads out to sea, look out world! He finds fish that snore, reels in the world's most expensive seafood dinner, and nearly drowns a classmate he was just trying to welcome to the islands.

Later in life he finds himself in trouble for fishing on a private beach. Of course George being George, he doesn't take this lying down. Together with other native Hawaiians he plays a role in establishing a law that has outlawed private beaches in the state. Meanwhile, he gets hold of some mysterious "magic" seeds and becomes Hawai'i's top grower of cucumbers and ginger before it all falls apart.

As with the first book, it's been a privilege and a delight to work with my good friend George on these wonderful stories. I trust that you'll enjoy them.

— *Paul Konwiser*

George Kahumoku, Jr.

# Acknowledgements

The authors of this book had lots of help and we are grateful. Helen Bigelow has been a dear friend and a guiding light for us, always. Sandy Miranda, who was so encouraging for our first book, was there for us once again. George's old friend Wayne Wong has provided guidance and inspiration and is now immortalized in this book. Nancy Kahumoku has worked with us on all aspects of the book and she is a big part of George's life and his stories. Sandy "Sweetie" Wales has worked closely on the development of the book as Publisher of Kealia Press.

# Da Stories

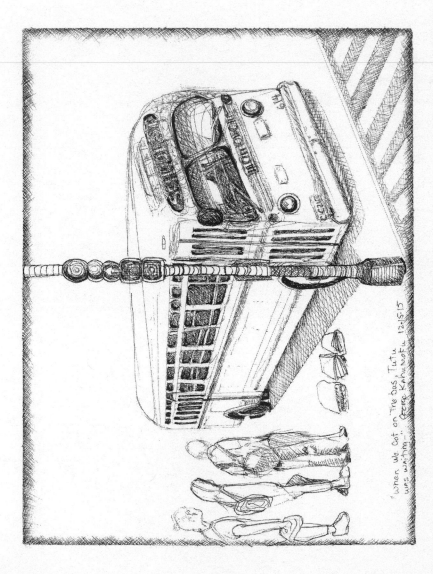

# Kung Fu Tutu and the Hymns of Hawai'i

As I was growing up, religion was a big part of my life. My aunties and my *tutu* (grandmother), always dressed in their finest, took me to church every Sunday. At our Kamakuamauloa Protestant church the sermon was in Hawaiian and we sang Hawaiian hymns. I might have been a little squirmy at having to be cooped up indoors on a nice day, but I sure loved the music. And it was not just in church where I heard this music while growing up. We used to sit around the kitchen table or our parlor at home, singing wonderful hymns. Sometimes we would sit outside at night under our neighbor's mango tree for what we called

17

*ohana* or family time. Each of us would share a *pauku* (Bible verse) like *Aloha I Ke Kahi I Ke Kahi* (Love One Another) or *Aloha Ke Akua* (God is Love). Some of the hymns we sang were written for Hawai'i by the Reverend Lorenzo Laimana Lyons, and had Hawaiian words from the beginning. Others had been originally written in English and translated into Hawaiian later. Regardless, I loved them all.

Back in small kid time, I lived with my *tutu* Emily Lihue Ho'opale Dulay while attending Kamehameha School. She also loved these old songs, and when I began my musical career many years later she thought I should record some of them. I thought so too, but what with one thing and another, I never seemed to get around to it. Whenever I saw my *tutu*, who was by then in her 80's, she would almost always ask me about recording the special hymns of our ancestors. She even lifted a hymnal from her church and gave it to me as a reminder. I always answered in the typical Hawaiian way, "*bom by, tutu, bom by*". I guess "*bom by*" is a sort of pidgin for "by and by." What it really means is a lot closer to the Spanish "mañana," which could mean anything from tomorrow to next week to "don't worry, I'll get around to it someday." Anyway, the years went past, and *tutu* got older and more frail, and finally she moved into the Sam Mahelona old folks' home on Kaua'i, the island where she had been born.

I used to go and visit her there whenever I could. In this place family visits were often in big groups, with 20 or 30 grandkids. I always brought my guitar with me, and *tutu* just loved to talk and sing. But little by little she started to lose both her physical and her mental faculties. After a while she couldn't walk anymore, but she still talked and sang. We used to push her around in a wheelchair. I would always give her a *lomi* massage. Then I didn't see her for a while, and I heard from my family that she couldn't even sit up any more, and she was confined to a bed.

I met Daniel Ho, the young Hawaiian musician, in 1999. After we had played together at a number of live performances, Daniel asked me if I would be interested in doing an album of Hawaiian hymns with him, sung with Hawaiian words. I have to tell you that this is when I knew I had found a musical partner. Finally, I was going to do an album of the hymns that I had been collecting for years. We did the recording with ten beautiful songs and released it as "Hymns of Hawai'i." Tutu Emily was 96 years old when I finally finished her album!

I couldn't wait for a chance to tell my *tutu* about it. Finally I made a trip to Kauai, and went over to the nursing home. "Your *tutu* has changed a lot," the nurse told me. "Don't be too shocked by what you see. Her mind is pretty much gone, and she doesn't communicate with anyone." The nurse said that she also was now completely bed-ridden.

The nurse showed me to *tutu's* room, and there she was, her small, lean form lying under a sheet in a bed. She looked up at me, but I couldn't tell if she recognized me or not. It was hard to see her like that. She was 97 years old, but it was still kind of a shock to me. As the nurse left the room, she said to me, "Your *tutu* is very special to us here. She's a real fighter."

That nurse was right, but she didn't know the half of it. The thought of *tutu* as a fighter took my mind back to a much earlier time. I was in first grade and my brother Van was in second. We were attending Kamehameha School, and living with Tutu Emily in the Pauoa Valley, two valleys away from Kalihi Valley, where the school was. Every day *tutu* would drop us off at the school bus stop on her way to work as a cook at Waimanu Home. After school, we were on our own. To get home, we took the Kamehameha private school bus to a stop called the Terminal on School Street. There we could catch the public bus to get back home to Pauoa Valley.

*Tutu* would give each of us bus fare and also a nickel to buy a snack after school from one of the Chinese stores located at the entrance to Pauoa Valley on Kanealii Avenue. From Square Deal market on the Nuuanu side, we could get shave ice with a scoop of vanilla ice cream and some azuki sweetened beans in two colors. They had red (strawberry) or blue (vanilla) flavor for 5 cents. Or we could go across the street to Chun & Tongs and get chow fun noodles for our nickels. The chow fun noodles were delicious, with bits of char siu pork, carrots, string beans, bean sprouts and onions with green onions and slices of scrambled egg tossed with the noodles and oyster sauce.

This was our daily routine for the first couple of months of school, but one day there was a change for the worse. A couple of stops after we got on the public bus, a bunch of kids from Mayor Wright Housing got on. These kids attended a middle school. They were around 12 or 13 years old, and there were around 6 or 7 of them. They were real bullies. They would harass my brother and me and push us around. On this day, my brother didn't realize that we were at their stop, and he was sitting in his seat happily flipping his nickel up and down in the air. The kids saw this and they came to our seat and parted Van from his nickel. Then they picked me up and *huli maka* flipped me upside down and stole my nickel, too.

From that day on it was the same routine every afternoon. These kids would get ahold of us and turn us upside down and shake us until the nickel fell out of our pockets. They let us know that if we told on them we would get an even worse licking. So no more shave ice or chow fun for us. The bus driver didn't want to get involved with these kinds of disputes – boys will be boys, I guess he figured. Anyway, he didn't do anything to help us.

One day Van decided that he was tired of getting hijacked and he fought back, so they really pushed us around and we both ended up on the filthy bus floor. At Kamehameha, we wore uniforms of pale khaki pants and white shirts. At home that night, *tutu* saw how dirty our uniforms were. She was mad! She told us if we kept getting our uniforms so dirty, she was going to give us both a licking. Van and I were much more afraid of a licking from *tutu* than a licking from those kids, so we had to tell her what had been happening to us.

We really didn't think she could do anything about the bully boys, but the very next day after school when we got on the HRT public bus, we got a big surprise. There was *tutu*, sitting in one of the seats! Now when *tutu* took time off from work, it was only for serious business. We walked to where she was sitting, and she told us to go sit where we usually sit. We went towards the rear of the bus, and she got up and took a seat one row behind us. She leaned over and told us to pretend not to know her. Not know her?! How does a little boy pretend not to know his own *tutu*? It was hard for us! Van and I sat there as we rode along, getting closer and closer to the stop where the bullies got on. We didn't say a word to each other. In fact we hardly dared to look at each other. We were really worried about what was going to happen when our little old grandmother came up against this tough bunch of hoodlums. As the bully stop grew nearer and nearer, Van and I were squirming in our seats, with one eye on *tutu* and the other focused on the front of the bus. We were scared, for ourselves and for our *tutu*.

When the bus stopped and the bullies got on, they immediately spotted us. If you ever go diving for lobster in a cave, one antenna of the lobster is always on you and the other is on the *puhi* (eel) in the cave. That's how our eyes were. One eye on the boys and one eye on Tutu! They walked back to where we were seated and started pushing us around, as usual. They didn't pay any attention to the little old lady sitting right behind us. They should have.

You might picture my *tutu* as a little old Hawaiian church lady in a colorful *mumu*, *lauhala* straw hat and nut lei. She was all that, but *tutu* had always known how to take care of herself. Her father was a successful business-man who had gone broke in the 1930's crash. She had survived the depression and had done very well for herself. She had always been a fit and active person. She also came from a long line of warriors. It was her great, great, great, great Uncle Kekuhaupio who had taught Kamehameha the Great the art of *lua* or Hawaiian martial arts. She was born into a family with 13 sisters in China Town where they grew up bootlegging and making 180 proof *okole hau* from the *ti* leaf root. There were no boys in the family. All 13 girls grew up to be street fighters in downtown Honolulu. And they looked after their own.

So the bullies were pretty surprised when suddenly this little old lady arose from her seat and walked quickly up behind the biggest kid. She grabbed his shoulder and spun him around. The kid was angry. "Who the f... are you lady?" Then he gave her the finger. Big mistake! I knew about *lua*, but this was the first time I'd seen it used. *Tutu* grabbed his upraised finger, stuck it up his nostril and flipped him against the back window of the bus. Bam! Another kid went flying down the aisle and landed on the floor. Bam! Before any of the other kids could react, she came at them, all arms and elbows and knees. Before our astonished eyes, our *tutu* had turned into a ninja lady: Kung Fu Tutu! To make a long story short, inside of a minute there were 7 hurting bully boys, lying all around the bus holding on to their crotches and their noses. She told them if they ever bothered us again, she would be back.

But she wasn't done. The bus driver had pulled over because of the commotion in the back. He probably thought the boys were attacking a little old lady. He was wrong. Seeing the kids lying around he demanded, "What's going on here, lady!?" With a flying kick in the air, she nailed him in the chest and head and knocked him down, dazing him. She picked him up by his nose and sat him down in a seat. Then she got right in his face. "These are my grandsons, and no one touches them. You'd better be looking after them from now on." Van and I sat there with our jaws hanging down. We were two stunned little boys. This was our *tutu*! Wow!

She calmly took a seat and when the driver recovered, he drove off. The boys limped off a couple of stops later at Mayor Wright housing, and *tutu* got off on the following stop, to catch a bus back the other way and retrieve her car.

For the next ten years, we always had the same bus driver. He had us sitting in front in the handicapped section, where he could keep an eye out for us. We rode the bus that way until we finally got our driver's licenses. Apart from an occasional stink eye from those kids, nobody ever bothered us again. They wanted nothing to do with Kung Fu Tutu.

So yes, Tutu Emily was a fighter all right. The day I went to tell her about the Hymns album, I couldn't seem to get any sort of response from her, so I went out to my car and brought back my guitar. You never know, but music is a good way to communicate. I wanted her to hear the hymns I'd recorded.

I started playing and singing, and she just lay there in a fetal position with no reaction at all. I felt pretty bad about how long "*bom by*" had become. Now it was too late. I had waited too long. Then I noticed that there was movement under the sheet, where her feet were. I stopped playing, because I thought she had developed a twitch and I might need to call the nurse. I noticed that as soon as I stopped playing, her foot stopped moving. So I started playing again. After a minute or so, her foot started twitching again. This time I could see that she was keeping time with the music with her foot. I kept on playing, and she started to open her mouth and make some little sounds. She was trying to sing along with me! One of the nurses heard me singing, and stopped to listen. She got really excited when she saw what *tutu* was doing. She yelled down the hall to the other nurses, "Hey, look at this. Auntie Emmy is singing." Everybody came running. This was the most action they had seen out of her 2 years. Everybody's eyes were filled with tears, including mine.

Tutu Emily passed away a few months later. I was sorry I had waited so long to record her favorite songs, but at least I was still in time to bring my *tutu* some small special gift to thank her for all she had done for me throughout my life. I hope you'll someday have a chance to attend a real Hawaiian church service and hear the wonderful music that inspired me as a child and continues to inspire me. And when you see the rows of little old church ladies in their *lauhala* hats, please say a prayer for my *tutu* Emily Lihue Ho'opale Dulay, aka Kung Fu Tutu.

George Kahumoku, Jr.

28

# Elementary Education

B ack in the 1950's, when Hawai'i was still a territory, it was not so easy for a young Hawaiian boy from a traditional rural background to get himself integrated into modern life on the islands. As tough as it was sometimes, I stuck it out. There were many of us in the same situation, but some couldn't do it. I especially remember Kanialu, my best friend in elementary school. He was another wild Hawaiian kid like me, but he was unable to cope. This is my story about how I was shaped by my experience at Kamehameha elementary school. My teachers made all the difference, and I learned something from all of them, even if some of the stuff was bad.

In 1950, my family was living in South Kona on the island of Hawai'i, and that's where we had always lived. Life there was rural and we all lived mostly in the old Hawaiian ways, with water catchment, and no electricity or indoor plumbing. But my *tutu* wanted all of her grandkids to take advantage of every opportunity, so she arranged for everyone to move to Oahu so that we all could attend Kamehameha Schools, a private school for

Native Hawaiians. Unfortunately, as it turned out, only two of us out of the 26 cousins were accepted, me and my older brother Van. The rest of the 24 cousins attended public schools in the Pauoa Valley, where we lived.

Kamehameha Schools admits only children of Native Hawaiian ancestry. A lot of people would assume that we would be taught about Hawaiian culture and values such as hula, Hawaiian language, things like that. But in 1955 when I started kindergarten there, it was just the opposite. What they wanted to do was to assimilate us into American society. They taught us everything but Hawaiian culture. Almost none of the teachers were Hawaiian. In fact, it was at Kamehameha that I met my first *ha'oles*.

Hawaiian language at school wasn't encouraged, and it wasn't taught or spoken either. Hula was strictly forbidden. One time my cousin Faith was at school, just sitting at her desk with her pigtails and missing front teeth, making a few hula moves. The teacher spoke sternly to her about "pagan" (a new word for me) Hawaiian dancing. Faith was suspended for two weeks. And she wasn't even standing, just making a few motions. We were only seven years old and we didn't understand it. But it did have an impact on me and I remembered it.

Those teachers were mostly from places like Alabama and Kentucky and Michigan. I heard that these places were on something called the Mainland. At the time, I didn't know where the Mainland was. All I knew is that it wasn't Hawai'i. So we weren't there to learn Hawaiian culture. But those teachers were kind. There was Mrs. Cundy, Mrs. Kreiger and many others. I especially remember Mrs. Moorehead because she was a redhead from Alabama. That was something I'd never seen before, red hair. We always invited each new teacher to our house, Hawaiian style. I remember that Mrs. Moorehead came to dinner and we had just a regular meal, no big deal, kalua pig, lomi salmon, *poi*. She ate everything. Then one time she invited us to her house in the teacher's cottages by the Bishop Museum and she opened up a can of cold chili beans. I'd never had a can of chili beans. I mean, we ate canned pork and beans but we cooked it with bacon, onions, brown sugar, ketchup and mustard, but this was cold chili beans straight from the can! And she gave us each a hot dog with no bun! I think she didn't know how to cook. What really shocked me was that she smoked. She said, "Do you mind if I smoke?", and my brother Van and I looked at each other like, "Wow, she's smoking." I'd never seen a teacher smoke before. My Auntie smoked, but I didn't think a teacher would do that.

Mrs. Violet Rosehill was our music teacher for my entire six years of elementary school. She was a Hawaiian, but was classically trained in opera. She taught us a few Hawaiian songs, but was somewhat unfamiliar with the Hawaiian language and the meaning of the songs she taught us. She taught us tunes that she liked. One of them that I remember was *"Koni au I ka Wai"*, which translates to, "I Throb for Liquid." It's a drinking song composed by our Merrie

Monarch, King David Kalakaua. There's a verse in there that speaks of urinating off a cliff. We all were clueless about what we were singing about. When we went home and started singing it for our family, my *tutu*, who spoke Hawaiian, was pretty surprised at what they were teaching us at school.

At home there was always a lot of action and things going on, but our *tutu* was strict in a pretty free-form way that allowed and encouraged each of us kids to be creative and still be individuals. At Kamehameha, for the first time in my life, there was structure. We had these workbooks, and what color workbook you were using told the story of how you were doing in school. You could tell how smart you were depending on the color of the workbook you were assigned. If you were assigned the red workbook, all of us classmates knew you were considered among the smartest in the class. If you weren't so smart you would be using the yellow book. I was always in the brown workbook, because I didn't know how to write and I couldn't read that well. Most of the other kids were from the city, but we were from the country. I could read verses from our Hawaiian Bible, but not English. But you just go through it and do whatever you have to do, no matter the color of your workbook.

It was when I hit fourth grade that things really turned a corner for me. My classroom teacher was Mrs. Esther Waihee McClellan. She was my first Native Hawaiian teacher. She was the Auntie of our past Governor Waihee, the first native Hawaiian governor of the state. She didn't use the colored workbooks, and she didn't put us in categories. I said to myself, I can learn from this *wahine*. She knew how to deal with someone like me. She treated us as individuals and we weren't stigmatized by the color of a workbook. Mostly she taught us all how to think for ourselves and develop relationships with each other through play, pretending, storytelling, food and art.

I needed a lot of attention, and she gave it to me. When I started acting up she would tell the whole class, "OK, class, George needs attention. Go for it George!" So I would get it out of my system, whatever it was, and then she would say, "OK, that's that. Can we get back to the lesson now?" This happened three of four times a day. I can't really remember what it was that I did. Maybe I was just a little over enthusiastic. She knew how to deal with me whereas the other teachers didn't. She was a little too late for my best friend Kanialu. He got kicked out of school for discipline problems in the third grade. If he had made it to fourth grade and had Mrs. McClellan, he would have been okay.

Mrs. McClellan set up all these different learning stations – one for painting, one for history, one for math, another for reading and so on. We made kites, candles, cracked mango seed, pickled mangos – stuff we'd do at home. We also did artwork, just about everything. We even had classes in hula and chanting in the old *kahiko* style. We put on a performance of the *Makahiki* season for the entire elementary school. There was a big old hall with stadium type seating just above our classroom in Bishop Hall. It wasn't used much, so we spent a lot of time dusting and cleaning it all up for the Makahiki performance. It was all in the Hawaiian language, which was new to many of the students. This was the first time we were able to use Hawaiian language in school. My dad had traveled to Tahiti and he brought back a couple of *pa'u* drums, so I was a drummer for the presentation.

Our fourth grade class was the only one doing things like this. The other fourth grade teacher was a *haole* lady named Mrs. Bonebreaker. That was her real name, but she was a kind lady. If anybody could break bones it was Mrs. McClellan. But she didn't have to. We all loved her and followed her lead. Fourth grade opened up my life. I saw that here was a Hawaiian who was also a teacher, and I thought to myself that maybe I could someday be a teacher too. She made everyone feel special. I know that there were 25 others in the class, but she made me feel like she was speaking only to me, not to 25 other kids.

We graduated to fifth grade and returned to the Main Campus, where we had much smaller classrooms for the same number of kids. Fifth grade was miserable with a teacher I didn't like at all. But the thing that saved me in fifth grade was art with Mrs. Lois Horn. She was the greatest. She would demonstrate a new art technique for about ten minutes and then just turn you loose and let you go for it. You had to think for yourself and problem solve the new media. She came to the classroom with her little cart and we made drawings and collages using pen and ink. I never had that kind of material at home. Our stuff at home was just sticks, and writing or drawing in the sand. Now I had paper. Paper wasn't important in our family for some reason, and we never had paper around. For me having paper was a big deal. Once they busted out paper I went through reams and reams of the stuff. For the other kids it wasn't anything special, but for me it was, "Wow, paper!" I'd draw on the front, I'd draw on the back, I'd draw on the sides, I'd fill the whole thing up. I'd just draw and draw for hours. The only thing I hated was when you had to clean up because then I knew that the day's class was over.

Gerald Meek was another teacher who influenced me and taught me how to think. I had him for art for grades 6, 7, and 8. He was just like Mrs. McClelland but he was a *haole*. He thought I had talent, but I also think he saw in me a kind of wild streak that we had in common. He let me do stuff no one else in the class was doing. He introduced me to batik. He had me doing ceramics. He put me on the potting wheel one time, and from that experience I knew I wanted to do this for the rest of my life. He showed me books by sculptor Henry Moore and all these other guys, Matisse, Cezanne, Dali, Picasso, whatever. I had no idea what I was doing. I made cubist stuff with blocks of clay. I'd just stack them together and he let me go crazy. He even lent me oil paint and taught me how to stretch canvasses that I took home. On weekends I'd go out to Kewalo Basin where my Dad worked for the U.S. Fish and Wildlife, and I'd draw and paint the boats in the harbor there.

At a young age, I watched my grandfather Willy Kahumoku carve canoes out of Koa logs he cut down himself. Grampa Willy would make *poi* boards out of felled *ulu* (breadfruit) trees and carve *poi* pounders out of stone that had reached the sea. Finally, I could see a connection between what I had learned at home and what I was being taught at Kamehameha Schools. I discovered this connection through the arts. I learned how make something out of nothing using only your own imagination, raw materials and subject matter you found in nature. Using your own two hands and hard work you could create something out of nothing. I was on my journey towards becoming an independent thinker, a hard worker, and an artist.

In kindergarten through 5th grades Miss Caroline Curtis, an old white haired lady, would come around once a week and tell us stories. She was very small, not much taller than us. Man, I looked forward to that once a week session of her story telling! And I really hated it when the other kids weren't paying attention or were talking. I was brought up by my family in the story telling tradition. It was something we did nearly every night after an evening meal. It's almost like going to church. And if somebody disturbs that they get told, "Shaddap!" Miss Curtis did story telling for all the classes, and it always impressed me that she carried around these notes scribbled in pencil on little pieces of paper so she would know where to pick up the story from last week. And the stories were Hawaiian stories, like the ones my *tutu* would tell: Stories about Pele and Kamapuapa and fishing stories, and catching ahi tuna using magic lures made from mother of pearl, like the ones that my dad made by hand. She gave us a wonderful glimpse or our connection to our Hawaiian culture. Miss Curtis was not Hawaiian, but she was kind of like a Hawaiian with a *ha'ole* body.

Most important for me, Miss Curtis taught me how to listen and imagine and visualize stories like full length movies in full multi-3-D color with Full Dolby surround sound! She taught me how to use my mind and imagination. She reinforced my *tutu's* visionary advice: if you see it in your mind, taste it, hear it ahead of time, it's yours. You can become whatever you envision and create your own destiny. This was the *huna* or secret of life. And I was learning it from Miss Curtis.

As I look back half a century later, I can see clearly how Kamehameha Schools was a mind-blowing transformation for me. I had some great teachers and some duds, both *haole* and Hawaiian. Through them, I developed a love of art and story-telling that is still with me today. I learned what it is to be a good quality teacher.

Over the years, I have often thought of my friend Kanialu. With the right kind of teacher he might have been able to take advantage of the opportunities that were just around the corner. I came so close to missing them myself. I think that what I have brought to teaching is the ability to use my Hawaiian cultural background to reach my students.

# The Chinese Cemetery

Several years ago I met famed ukulele artist Bill Tapia for the first time. Uncle Bill was almost 100 years old then and, like me, he enjoyed telling people stories from his life. Another thing that we found we had in common was that we both grew up in the Pauoa Valley. I was born in Kealia on the Kona side of the Big Island, but when I was accepted to Kamehameha Schools, I moved to Oahu so I could attend. Beginning from when I was five years old I lived with my grandparents on Kanealii Avenue in the Pauoa Valley. It's less than a mile from downtown Honolulu, but a world apart. Uncle Bill brought back some memories when he spoke about something he did as a child.

On the slopes of the Pauoa valley there is a Chinese cemetery. Chinese cemeteries are usually located on hillsides because this is supposed to improve Feng Shui. The Chinese have their own way of doing things, and this includes funerals. Improper funeral arrangements can cause ill fortune and disaster on the family of the deceased. One of the customs was to leave a bunch of food on the grave to feed the deceased on his journey to another world.

We Hawaiian kids living in the valley were on high alert whenever we saw a funeral procession going into the cemetery. There was a stone wall at the edge of the cemetery and 20 or 30 kids would be sitting on it in the shade of a plumeria tree waiting for the signal, which was the sound of firecrackers going off. At a Chinese funeral they would set off firecrackers when the funeral was over. I've heard that it's done to scare off bad spirits and bring good luck to the departed. I don't know about that. For us kids it meant that we were about to have some good luck ourselves. As soon as the last car left, we were at the grave sharing in the bounty.

Us kids could hear those firecrackers from anywhere in the Pauoa valley. Those were the sounds of whole roast duck, manapua (Chinese dumplings filled with sweet meats, shrimp or azuki sweetened beans), noodles, oranges, custard pies, sweetened baked and steamed dumplings and lots of other special treats. Sometimes there was even a whole roasted suckling pig. Often there even were coins wrapped up in ceremonial red paper. It would usually be a nickel, but sometimes there was a dime or even a quarter. This was big money for us. For a nickel you could go to the Square Deal Market and get the "superdeluxe" shave ice (red or blue) with azuki beans in the bottom. Or even a chow fun from Chung & Tongs. We hit the grave as soon as the mourners cleared out. We never got into trouble about this and some good food didn't go to waste (as far as we were concerned).

It turns out that back in Uncle Bill's time, he and the other neighborhood kids had been doing the exact same thing as I did. That's a span of three generations. I have to wonder if they're still doing the same thing today.

FOOD PRICE LIST

Dinner Rice — $2.50
BBQ stick — $.10
Chili Bowl w/Rice — 1.00
SAiMiN — 1.00
Spam Musibi/Hot Dog — .50
Andogs - Pu Gng 1 Dog — 1.00
Canned Juice & Soda — .25
ICE CAKE — .10
Shave ice — .05
Coffee 2 — .10
Tea — .5
Daikon
Rice Ball

"WE Went to ALL THE CELEBRATIONS TO SHARE! CULTURE & FOOD & MUSIC" George Kahumoku 2015

# A Taste of Religion

People go to church services for various reasons, I suppose. I think that you can learn more from church attendance than just the gospel. As a child I lived on Oahu in Pauoa Valley near what we called "church row." I had two brothers and 26 cousins who lived nearby in the valley. We weren't exactly poor, but we didn't hesitate to accept a helping hand, either. Every Sunday, my family would dress us in our Sunday best. We would put on our white dress shirts and khaki pants and even ties from our Kamehameha school uniforms. We also wore shoes and socks, because we knew we'd be walking all day. Then we'd set out for church. We weren't interested in church services so much as the food that the churches served.

First, we went to the Catholic Church. At 6 A.M. they served pancake breakfast with Log Cabin syrup and butter, and hot chocolate. By 11:30 we were at the Mormons, who served tuna sandwiches and orange exchange juice, which was supposed to be one can of concentrate to five cans of water. The Mormons thinned it down to 1 can concentrate to 10 cans of water. We didn't care. There was lots of ice and it was nice and cold and welcoming in that hot stuffy Mormon church next to the humid Auwaiolimu Stream. And there were chips!

From 2 to 4, the Filipino Holy Roller Church across from Booth Park on Kanealii Ave served boot boot, coconut sweetened rice steamed in banana leaves. And they gave us delicious Filipino pastries like fried lumpia with Filipino bananas in a fried wrap dusted with powdered sugar. Yummy!

We also attended the once a month Luau on Saturdays at Kamakuamauloa Protestant Church in Kalihi, where my Tutu Emily Lihue Hoopale Dulay was a Deacon. They served the Hawaiian standards: *laulau*, *poi*, white rice, kalua pig, chicken long rice, *lomi* salmon, *poke* fish, squid luau, and macaroni potato salad (made with Best Food Mayonaise, of course!) For desert there was *haupia* coconut pudding and sometimes *kulolo* (grated taro-coconut and brown sugar steamed in *ti* leaves).

The churches didn't feed us only on Sundays. We went to the MIA Boy Scout Tuesday night services every week at the Mormon Church where they served more juice with animal cookies. And every October there were the Harvest Bon dances of the Buddhist Church on Nu'uanu Avenue where they served sushi, rice balls, daikon and other pickled veggies.

Looking back on it, I have to say that even though I was not going for the services, I learned an appreciation for a charitable helping hand that is still with me today. We were kind of a mob of kids, but the churches expected us and were always kind and welcoming. And in church

46

I learned wonderful music that I finally got to record in my "Hymns of Hawai'i" album. I'll always be grateful for what I received and what I learned.

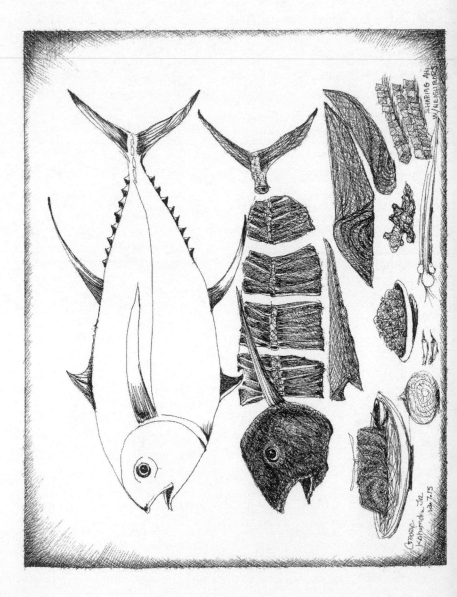

# Million Dollar Ahi

Sometimes our Hawaiian traditions come into conflict with the modern world. Being brought up in traditional Hawaiian ways, my brothers and I were steeped in the ideas of self sufficiency and sustainable living. My ancestors knew that if you didn't feed yourself, you starved. They had no contact with the outside world and no supermarkets to buy food. We raised what crops would grow in our climate and soil. And of course, we hunted and we fished.

When I was around eleven years old, my brother Van and I would go fishing several times a week. We lived in Pauoa Valley, which isn't all that close to the ocean. We would hop on our bicycles and ride down the hill for an hour or so to reach the beach.

One of the places that we liked to fish was off the pier in the Kewalo basin on the Ewa side of the Ala Moana park. We liked to go there because we didn't have to compete with other fishermen. That was because there was a particular pier that was closed to the public, but my dad was a diesel mechanic for the U.S. Division of Fish and Wildlife, and they had two large boats moored there. My dad worked on one of the boats, called the "Gilbert", and he would let us in. Then he'd usually go down into the ships' holds leaving Van and me with the place to ourselves.

One evening we were there fishing but not catching much, just a couple of *upupalu* (great for eating raw) and a bunch of pan sized silver *'ahole'hole* and stripped *mamo*. We had cheap, lightweight six pound test lines with BB shot weights attached, and #6 hooks for our homemade bamboo poles. We ate what we caught, and we knew that our family would be waiting for us to come home with our catch. With the sun going down and very little to show for a day fishing we decided to look around the facility. There was a chain link fence and behind it were what looked like covered holding tanks of some kind. We made sure that no one was around, and then we scaled the fence and walked over to check out the tanks.

The closest tank had a window in it so you could see underwater, and Van and I went over and peeked in. That's when we saw a most wonderful sight! It was a big ahi tuna, easily 20 or 30 pounds. He was swimming around the tank all by himself. He sure looked tasty. We scrambled back over the fence and then returned to the dock with our fishing lines hoping to catch a small bait fish to get that big ahi. It wasn't long before we had a perfect sized *'ahole'hole* on the hook. Back across the fence with our gear and our fresh bait. We found a place where we could climb up on the edge of the holding tank and hang our line inside. The ahi went right for our bait and immediately broke the line. He was just too heavy for our gear.

Not a problem. We knew where they kept the fishing gear on the Gilbert and we swiped a couple of big hooks and some heavier line. We also got a couple of large bamboo poles perfect for a good sized ahi. We scaled the fence once again, this time with our heavier tackle and fresh bait. We climbed up the feeding station and up to the tank. We used both of the heavy poles, with our bait on the middle jig between them, and lowered the bait into the tank. In less than a minute, BAM! we hooked him and we had the fight of our lives. We had him hooked good! We worked him, just as we had seen our dad and other fishermen do hundreds of times before when we went out with them fishing for ahi, *aku* and *kawakawa.*

Van and I hauled our catch out of the tank and dropped him on the asphalt parking lot surrounding the holding tank. This fish was a real fighter, and he kept on jumping around. With no fish bat, we grabbed some rocks and we kept clobbering him on the head until we finally killed him. We made quite a mess on the dock. There was a trash bin nearby with some cardboard and old newspapers stacked up inside. We got the newspapers and did our best to wrap up the fish in paper and cardboard. Then we had to boost him over the fence. We finally managed it and we got the sucker tied onto Van's bike rack. It took us nearly two hours to get back home to Pauoa valley. It's all uphill, and half of the time we had to push our bikes. But we knew we'd be heroes at home when we came in with our best catch ever.

And we were right. Everyone loved the fish. Our dad had taught us how to dress ahi, and all kinds of fish. We carefully slid our knife around the fins of the ahi and saved the head and tail and side and dorsal fins for soup along with the heart, kidneys, liver, stomach and intestines. We halved and skinned and filleted out the boneless fish meat, cut the center bone up with a cleaver and sliced off the two belly sides for frying. We cut up the fillets into long fish length slabs for raw sashimi and raw poke or cubed raw fish. There was plenty for everyone, and we shared with our neighbors Hawaiian style. Van and I took turns cutting the entire fish up. Half of the head, tail, side and dorsal fins with the heart and liver went to the Wongs, our Chinese family friends across the street. They used it for fish soup. Part of the sweet center bone and a section of the belly and part of a fillet went to Chinese and Portuguese neighbors, the Lau *ohana*, who lived *mauka* (mountain side) of our house. The Lau's used their portion for frying and making raw sashimi. Part of the belly along with another slab of the fillet, we shared with the Tom ohana, who lived next door *makai*-side (towards the ocean) of our house. The Toms used their portion of the fish for frying and making raw poke with onions, shoyu sauce, ginger, sesame seeds and onions. With what was left our Tutu Emily Lihue, made vinhadosh vinegar garlic Hawaiian salt fried fish, poke with *inamona* (*kukui* nut relish), and *limu kohu* (seaweed green) and Maui sweet onions and oyster sauce. She also made a platter of thinly sliced raw ahi sashimi, over a bed of finely shredded lettuce with a dipping sauce of hot spicy Chinese mustard and shoyu. Grampa Bonifacio Dulay, made Filipino fish soup (*sabau*) with the other half of the head and left over dorsal and side fins. He added garlic, ginger, sliced tomatoes, and onions with bay leaf and Patis-Filipino fish anchovies sauce with sliced choy chinese cabbage and dry land watercress with green onions from our garden. Everybody got the piece they liked. Our entire neighborhood smelled of fish cooking, and we feasted on this ahi for two days

A couple of days later my grandfather, who lived with us, was sitting at the breakfast table reading the newspaper. He was the only one in the family who read the paper, but we all knew what was going on the world because whenever he saw something interesting he would make an announcement and read the article out loud. On this day he found an article about a subject that he knew we cared about: fishing.

The article said that someone had broken into the F&W facility down in Kewalo basin and stolen an ahi that they had in a holding tank there. Van and I stole a quick look at each other but we kept our mouths shut. My grandfather kept on reading. Normally stealing a fish would not be news, but this fish was. He had been hand-raised by a team of scientists studying fish behavior. They had had the fish for nearly two years, and the team of scientists had invested about a million dollars in time and equipment as part of the study. This fish had been trained like a dolphin to respond to hand signals and retrieve rings from the bottom of the fish tank it was living in. Two years of fish training and studying fish behavior went down the drain. Wow! Van and I were shocked, but we swore ourselves to secrecy and we never fished there again.

This all happened more than fifty years ago, and it's the first time I've told this story. I hope that there is some statute of limitations so that Van and I won't be prosecuted after so many years. But there's something I'm more concerned about. I have become good friends with Tagay and Renee Kang. Tagay was a young scientist on the project team studying this particular ahi back in the early 1960's. Renee also knew my dad because she worked as a secretary for U.S. Fish and Wildlife at Kewalo Basin. They both called my Dad "Kokomo" and they were both fond of him. They're retired now, and living in Seattle. The Kangs have become my great friends over the last 20 years. They make it a point to come to my Napili show once every few years and they've seen me perform in the Seattle area. Somehow, I can't bring myself to gather the courage to tell them how we ate his million dollar experiment! I'm hoping he'll forgive a couple of dumb kids.

When I hear these days about pricey seafood dishes like bluefin tuna going for $100 a pound,

I'm impressed. Still, I think that back in the early 1960s we might have eaten the most expensive seafood dinner ever and we got to share that expensive meal with all our neighbors in Pauoa Valley!

Note: Months later, Van and I went to visit my Dad at Kewalo basin. At that time, there was a sign that said "Poison Fish" and there was barbed wire all over the top of the fencing we had scaled.

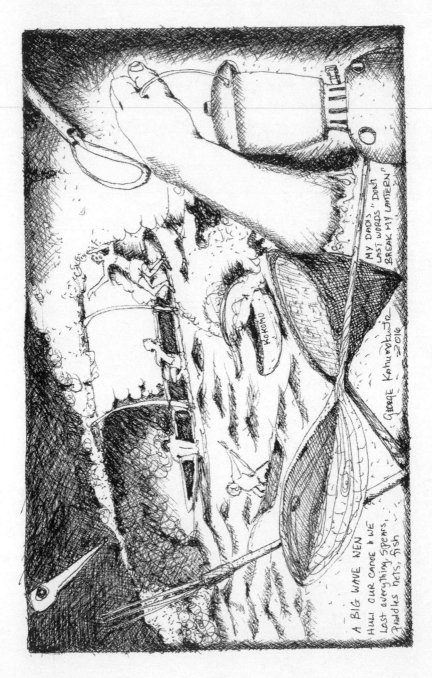

# E Komo Mai

## (How we nearly killed poor Jim Stonehill from Shaker Heights, Ohio)

*E komo mai* are words of welcome. We Hawaiians are known for our hospitality. It's a value that I grew up with. But sometimes we need to be more careful about how we extend that greeting. You can get yourself in trouble and risk a tragic outcome. This is the story of a close call for my friend Jim Stonehill, who somehow managed to survive our warm Hawaiian reception.

I became acquainted with Jim through my best friend in high school, Wayne Wong. I had met Wayne at the beginning of 6th grade in Kamehameha Schools. We both ended up in a speech therapy class that we had to go to instead of one of our regular classes. I was in the class because I failed the standard test they gave to kids who, like me, grew up speaking pidgin. The test was pretty simple. They had you count to three. If you answered, "One, Two, Three," you were in the clear. But if you said, "One, Two, Tree" — speech therapy. Wayne had excellent English pronunciation but he had new braces and couldn't pronounce the "th" sound either, so he was stuck in speech therapy too. We hated speech therapy but it was better than school. Our teacher was Mrs. Holden from Michigan. We spent the whole class repeating after Mrs. Holden words like "these," "those," "three" (instead of "tree"), them instead of "dem".

Wayne and I discovered that we had a lot in common. We both signed up for the diving team. We both tried out for football, but neither of us made the team. Wayne was fast, but he was small. I was big enough, but too slow. Mostly we spent our time in the water. We surfed every day before and after school. Wayne and I thought that we were pretty hot stuff on the waves. When I think back on it now, we weren't all that good. We weren't too good at making surfboards either. We tried to make our own boards but we messed up somehow and the resin didn't set up. It still hadn't hardened a year later, so we gave up on that. Later we found out about the effect of weather. When you apply fiberglass in a pouring storm in the middle of a rain forest you don't get a good result.

Later we got jobs, me pumping gas for Lippy Espinda in Waikiki and Wayne working as a bag boy at the old Chun Hoon supermarket on the corner of Nu'uanu Avenue and South School Street. Still, we were in the water at every opportunity. We had lots of surfing adventures, including getting arrested for surfing near the old wall in Waikiki. We got hauled away in a cop car still in our wet bathing suits. The police station was air conditioned and we sat in a cell singing songs to try to keep warm. It cost $35 for my dad to bail us out.

At Kamehameha Schools we had exchange programs with mainland schools. Wayne had been in Shaker Heights, Ohio for his junior year, and in our senior year we had a kid named Jim Stonehill from Shaker Heights show up in our school. It was an exchange program where Wayne lived with Jim for an entire school year in Ohio and in return, Jim came to Hawai'i to live with Wayne's family. Jim was a nice kid and Wayne and I thought it would be hospitable to have him join us on one of our ocean going expeditions, night fishing from a canoe.

Our canoe was a small outrigger, a 14 footer that belonged to my dad. It was really a two man canoe, so we were a little overloaded and out of balance with three people. We went out to Sunset beach, a surfing spot on the north shore famous for its huge waves during the winter months. But it was summer time and the waves were small. We had our paddles and spears, and we set out over the reef. My dad had lent us his gas lantern, which had a tiny nylon bag as a wick. You pump it up to get intense white light. It had been given to him by his grandfather Willy. I remember that the last thing he said to me when we left the house was, "Don't break my lamp." I planned to take good care of it.

Of course, we checked with Jim to make sure he could swim, just in case. He told us that he was a strong swimmer and we took him at his word. At around 10 P.M. we paddled out into a calm sea to about 300 yards from shore. We hung the lamp high over our heads on one side of the canoe to attract the fish. We didn't care

59

what type of fish we caught, and whatever came up is what we scooped into our net. Before long we found ourselves surrounded by a school of stickfish. We got plenty of them. We had the spears ready in case something larger turned up.

All went well for a while, but there then there was a sudden freak swell and we started getting hit by some pretty good sized waves. The canoe was rocking like crazy and it looked like it was going to overturn. I grabbed the spears and threw them as far away from the boat as I could manage. We didn't want to get stabbed with our own spears if the canoe flipped. Jim looked really scared and he was holding onto the gunwales for dear life. Finally it happened: A huge wave hit us broadside and we did a *huli maka* flip (capsized). The canoe went over and we were all in the water.

All I could think about was saving my dad's lantern. If it got into the water the hot glass was going to explode. Saving the lantern was the most important thing to me, so I was in the water holding the thing as high as I could over my head. The water was not deep, but Sunset is over a sharp reef filled with *wana* (sea urchins) with needle-sharp spines that could give you a nasty wound if you stepped on them. I had to tread water and try to get to shore while holding the lamp above my head with my right hand while treading water with my left hand and both feet circling beneath me while heading back to shore.

Wayne stuck with the canoe. When it flipped, the *ama* (outrigger) which is attached with twine, came loose and it disappeared into the night along with our paddles. Wayne was trying to save the canoe and I was trying to save my dad's lamp. Poor Jim was on his own, hanging on for dear life to what was left of our canoe. We weren't too worried about him because he had said he was a strong swimmer. Eventually we all got to the beach with the canoe, the lamp and Jim. Jim sat on the beach crying, I suppose in both fear and relief. That's when we found out that he had never been in the ocean before and all his swimming had been in a swimming pool!

Wayne's family owned a beach house nearby and we spent the night there. The next day we walked the beach looking for the outrigger and our paddles. We found them scattered along the beach two miles away.

So in the end, the canoe was saved, the lamp was saved, and Jim Stonehill somehow survived our friendly Hawaiian welcome to become an excellent surfer at home in the ocean. After that we called him Kimo Pohaku Pu'u (Jim Stonehill in Hawaiian), and for the rest of the school year he joined us almost every day on our surfing safaris.

George Kahumoku, Jr.

THE OLD PALI ROAD
WAS SCARY & DARK

George Kahumoku
2015

# A Flat Tire Changes My Life

I was in my senior year in 1969 at Kamehameha Schools where I had attended for going on almost 13 years, since kindergarten. I didn't much know what I was going to do after graduation. My older brother Van had gone into the army and he really liked it a lot. I had a lot of friends and cousins who were planning to go into the military too, so that seemed to be my destiny. These were the war years, so I thought my destiny lay in joining my *ohana* (family) fighting in Vietnam.

As a student growing up, I loved drawing and painting, ceramics and sculpture and would have liked to go to a college but that was out of my reach and out of the picture. For one thing, I couldn't afford it. And for another thing I didn't have a great school record. It wasn't just my grades - they were more or less okay. But I seemed to get called into the principal's office quite a lot. It was for pretty small stuff, mostly for being late for school.

My best friend Wayne and I would go surfing nearly every day before school, after school and on weekends when we weren't working. We always tried to get to school on time at 7:45 A.M. but sometimes the waves were pretty good and it just wasn't possible. Anyway, a call into the principal's office wasn't so unusual for me. However it was never the principal I saw. It was usually the Vice Principal or the Dean who ended up counseling or scolding me.

I was always short of money and always hustling to earn more. I started an auto detailing business and I also fabricated and sold aluminum products and home renovations. My Dad was a retired fisherman and diesel mechanic and I had done my own car repair for years. I worked for Lippy Espinda for years since I was 11 years old and then I got this job working part time at a Chevron station on the corner of Nuʻuanu Avenue and Pauoa and Booth Roads. It was once the home of the old Piggly Wiggly store on the way into Pauoa Valley where we lived. Once in a while I'd make a run in their tow truck to help out a driver in trouble.

One rainy night, I was working there at the Chevron and some guy drove in and told us that he had seen someone by the side of the road on the Old Pali Highway trying to get some help. It was pounding rain and I would have liked to stay inside, but decided that I should take a run up there to see if I could help the guy out. I jumped into the service truck and headed up the hill on Nuʻuanu Avenue towards the Old Pali Road. It was close to where my friend Wayne lived on Waokanaka Street and if I got into trouble I knew I could call on Wayne for help.

For your information, the Old Pali Road is a scary place during the day, even scarier at night, and even doubly worse scary on a stormy night. It's said to be a place where the Menehune, the magic small muscular people of old, and the Night Marchers, dead lost wondering souls of past unresolved dead warriors, hang out. People are warned about carrying cooked pig or pork on the Old Pali Road because the spirits would be *ono* (hungry) for the pig in your vehicle and somehow cause your vehicle to stall or even stop you from moving forward until you shared your pig with them, by throwing it (the pig or pork you were carrying) out the window of your car.

This may sound silly and superstitious to a non-Hawaiian, but for me there was a vivid memory from childhood that made me a believer. One night we were driving home from a *luau* in Waimanalo with my parents and grandparents. In our car was left over kalua pig, *lau laus* and filipino pork and peas with poke fish and poi. All was well until we turned onto the Pali Road and started down the hill. Suddenly our car stopped running and we came to a halt in the middle of the road. An argument started between my mom and dad. My mom told my dad to throw all that left over food out the window. My dad said that there was no way he was going to throw out our food. Then he got out of the car, walked round and round, and began shouting bad cussing words in Hawaiian to these Old Pali Road spirits. Basically what he said was, this was <u>his</u> kalua

65

pig, his *laulau* and his Hawaiian food and he wasn't about to give it up to any lost spirits. He called on our *ohana* or family spirits to fight the bad spirit guys. He said in Hawaiian that this food was his and he was staking his territory! Then he zipped open his pants, whipped his *uli* (you know) out and proceeded to urinate around the entire car so as to stake his claim. It was indigenous and very primal, but that was our way. When he was done, he got in the car, hit the ignition and our car started right back up!

So on that rainy night years later was I nervous as I headed up Nuʻuanu Valley and turned right onto the Old Pali Road? You bet I was! Long scary roots and shadows hung down from the Banyan trees along the roadside. About 10 minutes later I came up on this big black Cadillac on a curve on the side of the road. He had his emergency flashers going. I knew that there were a bunch of big old homes of wealthy people along this road, so the Cadillac was not surprising. I pulled up behind the car and an old man got out. He must have been around 80 years old. He had a flat tire and I told him I could fix it for him. He popped open the trunk from a button in the glove compartment and it didn't take me long to get the car jacked up with my big tow truck jack. I had the tire changed in around 15 minutes.

The rain had let up and the guy paid me cash for the service call, but I guess he saw that I was a Hawaiian kid, and for some reason he took an interest in me. He asked me my name and I said I was George Kahumoku Jr. Seeing my military style haircut, he asked me if I went to

Kamehameha Schools. I told him I was a senior and an officer from Company D and a Platoon Commander. He didn't know any Kahumokus so he asked me what my grandparents and great grandparents names were. When you're brought up the Hawaiian way, as I was, you learn your whole genealogy right back to Adam and Eve, practically.

Part of my upbringing includes having respect for your elders. Even though I would have liked to get in my truck and off of the Old Pali Road, he wanted the whole story. After reciting a few generations of names, I finally came up with one name that he knew: it was my grandmother, my Tutu Emily Ho'opale Dulay.

It turns out that this guy had a connection with her and her dad John Ho'opale, my great grandfather. I was surprised because he even knew my *tutu* by her Hawaiian name, Lihue. She was named after the place she was born and raised on Kaua'i. Because he knew my *tutu*, now he knew who I was. He also asked me a lot about my future plans, and I told him that I would like to go to art school, but would probably go into the army instead and join my brother in Vietnam. Now that he heard my story, he let me go and I headed back to the service station down. I thought to myself, what a *ni'ele* (nosey) man.

A couple of days later I got handed yet another pink slip notice to come to the principal's office. I hadn't been late to school for a while, but the weekend before, Wayne and I wanted to use the school woodshop for a project we were working on. We had climbed a fence and gone over to a locked area on our school campus. We busted in to use my art teacher Mr. Konishi's art room table saw. A table saw makes a lot of noise, but we didn't realize that there would be someone around. A security guard found us there. When we told him that we were students he said it was okay and he wouldn't rat us out. I think it also helped that we kind of bought him off with some food from Kenny's Burger House in Kalihi. You could get a Porky Bay sandwich for 99 cents, and we had a couple that we hadn't eaten yet so we gave them to the guy. He went off with the food, and we finished our work and left. But now I figured that he did rat us out because here I was headed for the principal's office.

As I walked slowly down the hall, my mind was working on all kinds of excuses for breaking into the wood shop and using the equipment. Disciplinary stuff was usually handled by Ms. Winona Reuben, the vice principal, or Mr. Dave Faust, the Dean. But when I got to the office this time, they sent me directly to the principal, Mrs. Gladys Brandt. It was she who wanted to see me. Mrs. Brandt was a no-nonsense, tough lady, and she was the only Hawaiian principal I had ever met in my life. I knew I was in trouble, because I couldn't pull a fast one on her. She was Hawaiian and I was Hawaiian. I respected her and couldn't lie to her because she would see right through me. This was the first time I was actually going to see her one on one. Right then and there I made a decision to tell her the truth, the whole truth, and nothing but the truth. I was scared!

I nervously sat down in the chair in front of her desk expecting the worst, and I figured it would be best to confess right up front. Once I got started talking I couldn't stop, I was so nervous. I was really running off at the mouth, trying to explain about the shop and our project and why we were there on the weekend, and how we would never do such a thing again without permission. Finally she interrupted me.

"What are you talking about?" she asked me. Obviously she was busy and had something to say to me, and wasn't interested in my babbling. So I shut my mouth and just looked at her. That's when she surprised me by smiling at me.

"Do you know who Richard Lyman is?" she asked me.

Of course I knew who he was. He was a trustee of the Bishop Estate as well as Kamehameha Schools. I knew the name well, but I'd never met him. He sometimes turned up at school assemblies, and at our yearly Song Contest. But sitting in the back of the auditorium with a thousand other kids anxious to bust out of school for the day I never paid attention to the panel of guys in suits and ties sitting on the stage a mile away.

"You don't remember meeting him?" she asked me.

"No," I told her. "I never did meet him."

"Oh, but you did," she said. "On the Old Pali Road. You changed his flat tire for him."

"What? That was him?" I asked. I guess I never got a good look at him in the dark rainy night on that old scary Pali Road. I was more interested in getting the heck out of there!

"Yes, and you made a big impression on him, evidently."

Then she told me something amazing. Richard Lyman had been impressed by my respectful behavior, and he had decided, since he knew my family, he wanted to do something special for me. Actually it wasn't just because of me. Mr. Lyman came from the Puna District on the Big Island. Early in his political career had been running to be a representative for a Territory of Hawai'i office. He needed to get better known on the Kona side of the island, where my family came from. My grandmother Emily Lihue Ho'opale, had taken a liking to him. She took him to all the family gatherings in Kona and played a key role in helping him get elected into the Hawai'i Territorial Legislature in the 40's and 50's.

On the day after I changed his tire, he had spoken about me to Mrs. Brandt, and they decided that I should go to art school instead of Vietnam and that he would arrange to help me pay for it. He offered to send me to any school on the mainland I wanted to attend. He would pay for the school, but I would have to pay for the trip to get there. I guess he wanted me to have some incentive.

I knew about the good art schools because I had looked at the catalogs and dreamed of going to one of them, even though I never thought it would really be possible. However with Richard

Lyman's direction and the assistance of Gerry Johansen and Fred Gross from the Kamehameha Schools Higher Education and Financial Aid Department, I was accepted to several schools, including Rhode Island School of Design, Kansas City Art Institute, Los Angeles Art Institute, and San Francisco Art Institute. In the end I chose the California College of Arts and Crafts in Oakland because Northwest Airlines had an $89 roundtrip all-you-can-drink champagne flight between Honolulu and Oakland. If things didn't work out, or I changed my mind, I could easily return home. Heck I didn't even drink champagne!

Five years later, I graduated with my bachelor's and master's degrees in the arts plus a California State Teaching Credential. All thanks to a lucky flat tire change on the Old Pali Road, a flat tire that changed my destiny.

# The Snoring Uhus of Holualoa Bay

*This story is dedicated to the legendary Auntie Nona Beamer. A few years ago she asked me to remind George about snoring fish so that the story could go into the next volume of "A Hawaiian Life." - PK*

I have a friend who likes to fish. He's a young guy who used to bartend at the Westin Ka'anapali and he spent all his spare time fishing and almost all his money on the latest fishing equipment. He had a fish finder, which is like a kind of sonar. He spent all kinds of bucks on special rods and reels and lots of other equipment. Not to mention the upkeep of his boat and motor and the yearly safety check for his boat trailer. To me, getting ready to go fishing with him seemed like setting up for a Mount Everest expedition compared to the way I learned to fish growing up in Kona.

When we were kids, my family and I would go out fishing with homemade torches in the rocks and shallow reefs in Holualoa Bay in Kona. We went torch fishing at night during the last quarter of the moon when the sky was darkest and the fish were sleeping. The whole family went, parents, grandparents, aunties and uncles, kids. We used torches to light the way and to attract the fish. We wore little rubber and canvas reef walkers called "tubbies," shaped like our feet and toes to keep from slipping on the lava rocks and to protect our feet from the sharp coral reef and the sharp points of the *wana* or sea urchin crawling around at night. Around our waists, we carried an old recycled 50 pound cotton rice bag with a sewed-on belt strap to put our catch in. In one hand we carried a homemade spear. These were straight wooden poles, 2 inches in diameter and 6 to 8 foot long, made from *lama* or strawberry guava wood with a sharpened metal three-pronged tip. We used them to spear the fish and also as a hanger to hang the fish in the rice bag when moving about the reef.

Because we were night fishing, we made torches out of 3 or 4 inch diameter bamboo poles. They were cut to around 3-4 feet in length, with the bamboo cylinder and cavity on top stuffed with a small torn piece of an old Kona coffee burlap bag that was soaked in kerosene. The burlap bag acted as a wick for our homemade torch when lit. We tucked the bamboo torch pole down the back of our shirt and into our shorts and with a piece of

74

cordage or rope tied the bamboo to hold it in place around our waist. The torch flame was burning just over our heads. Your head and hair would get really sooty. As the torch burned down it got closer and closer to your head and it started to singe your hair. You learned pretty quickly to recognize that smell of your hair on fire. Then you adjusted the torch a little higher.

I liked to try to catch parrot fish, which we know as *uhu*. The *uhu* is a nice sized fish, from maybe 5 up to 12 pounds with 1/2 to 1 inch beautiful colored scales. It has a tasty white meat with a texture and flavor pretty close to lobster. *Uhus* eat little shrimp and crustaceans and have a beak like a parrot, which they use to actually nibble off bits and pieces of the coral looking for food hidden there. Hawaiians believe that every piece of sand on the beach has gone through an *uhu*. The males are blue and the females are kind of reddish. They both taste about the same. However, the meat of the larger blue males is kind of rubbery, so you want to try to get the younger red females because the meat is more tender.

From my family, I learned the location of secret caves where the *uhu* go to sleep at night. *Uhus* always go to the *puka* (hole) where they nest. Even if you fish out that *puka*, another *uhu* will find it and move in. Then you could sneak up on them and spear them in the hole where they are sleeping. And we had a special way to find them.

*Uhus* emit a strong odor that can attract predators. At night, they create a bubble nest around their bodies that surrounds them and hides their smell. Then the *uhu* goes to sleep surrounded by these bubbles. The thing is, the bubbles cover their smell, but they also make a sound like the fish is snoring. What you would do is stick your head in the cave and just be very quiet and listen to find out if there were any *uhus* in there. If you knew what to listen for, you could hear them snoring! I tell people about this and they think I am kidding, but it's true - these fish really snore!

Another thing I learned about *uhu* is that they can change sex from a red female to blue colored male. I found this out from observing my pet *uhu*. I guess she wasn't really a pet. When I was about nine years old, and home for the summer in Kealia, I caught this small 1-1/2 pound female red *uhu* at Kealia beach in South Kona. The tide had gone out and this baby female red *uhu* was stuck in one of the small tidal pools, stranded. I already had enough fish that day, so I threaded and tied a 30 pound mono filament fishing line to her through her gills and under her chin and kept her in a rock pool just off shore in the shallow tide pools. The other end of the line, I fastened to a huge rock so she wouldn't run away. When I went back to get her later at high tide, I saw that there was another *uhu* in the pool. They were having an *uhu* confrontation. *Uhu's* are territorial, and if one *uhu* stays in a location another one comes along eventually to challenge her or him. So, I got out my spear and net and scooped up both fish. Then I speared and ate the new *uhu* who had challenged my "pet" fish. I put my pet red *uhu* back in the tide pool again kept it tied to my string looped through the underside of her gills. She could still eat and swim about in the shallow tide pools. A couple of days later I went back and sure enough, there was another *uhu* standoff going on. Again, I scooped them both up in my net, grabbed the other fish, and then returned my girl red fish back to the tide pool.

After that I checked on my fish nearly every day. Sometimes I would go down there and find that she had gotten her line tangled around herself or she was caught on the rocks and reef. I'd have to untangle her and free her up. It was kind of like a pet dog in a back yard getting tangled up in his line. As the summer months went by, I saw that she was gradually changing color from red to blue and pretty soon she had become totally blue and that she was now a he. Still, plenty of other fish came in to challenge. During those summer months, she helped me catch around 3 dozen other *uhus*. After that, I figured he (now a full grown 7 pound blue *uhu*) deserved his freedom and I untied my fishing line and set him free to go back into the wild.

I don't live on the Big Island now, but I visit there pretty often. Sometimes when I'm in Kona on a moonless night I'll see a bunch of people in the water night-fishing. Of course they have the latest spear guns, wetsuits, searchlights and battery powered headlamps. These are modern Hawaiians and they never have to worry about setting their hair on fire. But I would guess they don't know that right near by, *uhus* are asleep in hidden caves protected by their bubbled nests from other predators. And I'll bet they've never heard a fish snore.

A Hawaiian Life Volume 2

# Three Chickens, Four Lessons

*Na moa* or chickens have always been important to us Hawaiians. The early Polynesian voyagers brought chickens to Hawai'i on their canoes along with their various plants. Now, feral birds can be found everywhere in the islands. In captivity, we raise chickens for the protein they provide through their eggs and meat. Some people also use chickens to wager bets and for entertainment through cock fights. I've had chickens in my life ever since my *hanabata* days, small kid time. From when I was around 9 years old I raised chicks that I won at the Hawai'i State Fair. I also helped my Filipino Grandfather Maning Alagao care for over 200 fighting cocks on weekends on Oahu near the Filipino camp behind the old Waimanalo Theater.

I grew up in Kealia South Kona, but I was also raised on Oahu where I attended Kamahameha Schools for 13 years. In 1992, I moved to Maui to play music and ended up teaching school at Lahainaluna High School as well. In my 65 years of life, much of our islands have gone from a rural to an urban community. Along with us Hawaiians and local people, the chickens have also made this adaptation. Somehow we have all managed to survive the transition!

For me, waking up to the sound of crowing has always been a normal part of life. But not everyone feels that way about it. Today, there are more and more complaints about feral chickens, in particular about the noise of crowing roosters. We live in an agricultural subdivision with 20 chickens, 50 goats, 2 dozen sheep, over 100 ducks, 3 miniature horses, one dog and one cat. But there's a covenant in our homeowners association rules: NO roosters! However, the feral chickens continue to live in the wild and we can still hear them crowing in the distance. Once in a while a whole flock of feral birds, roosters as well as hens, will appear in our yard. I'll start trapping them to make chicken papaya for dinner or lunch!

A neighbor of mine noticed a bunch of small chicks on the road near his house. He decided to capture them so that he'd have a supply of eggs. He trapped eight of them in cages and took them home. The thing with baby chicks is that they all look pretty much alike when they are young. You can't tell one from another and you can't tell males from females without close examination. His birds grew up and it turned out that three of them were roosters. He found out when they started crowing at 2 a.m. every morning and waking him and his wife up. He didn't know what to do with the birds. Like most of my neighbors he's not a farmer and he had no clue as to how to slaughter and dress a chicken. He asked me if I wanted them.

I'd wanted to have some roosters for breeding my laying hens and I thought I had a way to keep them quiet. I learned a lot about chickens from my grandfather. He once showed me how you could make a small cut in a rooster's tongue and that would keep them from crowing. It was a pretty dim memory, though, and I didn't know how to make the cut exactly.

So what I did was try cutting the tongues of my three young roosters. I cut their tongues three different ways. Then I marked and trimmed each chicken comb three different ways so that I could tell the chickens apart and know which type of tongue cut worked. I cut one comb in a vee shape, one kind of circular and one straight across the top. That evening, I cut each young rooster's tongue a different way and then I waited for morning.

It worked! The next morning, all of the roosters were quiet and I was pretty happy. But within a couple of weeks, first one, then another, then all three started crowing again. I guess the slits I had cut all grew back. I knew I was going to have to get rid of them.

I have been raised to get maximum use out of everything so I decided to take those three roosters to Lahainaluna High School where they could be used to provide valuable education to my students. On a bright Hawaiian Wednesday morning I loaded them into three separate cages in the back of my old Toyota pickup truck and brought them to school.

These little yellow chicks had become three distinctly beautiful roosters. One was a bright pumpkin color, with yellow streaks and a black tail. Another had black and blue markings and a white tail, and the third was red with a beautiful blue-red tail with one white tail feather. I figured that they would be great for my art classes to sketch as part of a life drawing lesson.

I parked the truck in the driveway right below my classroom and the kids came out with their sketch pads and drew the birds with pencil and paper as part of the class lesson. All of my classes went through the drawing thing. On Wednesday and Thursday, we drew them for the first two periods of the day with two different art classes until 10 A.M. This was Lesson #1.

Friday was D-Day for the chickens: It was time for Lesson #2, biology. In our biology classes the kids normally dissected small frogs and things like that. I thought that dissecting a chicken would be better. That's when I think I'm at my best as a teacher, when I'm sharing stuff that's for real with the kids, real hands-on stuff.

So that Friday at period three, I killed the chickens and turned our art class into a biology and chicken anatomy class. I got help from the students who lived on a farm and were used to this. We said a little prayer thanking *Akua* (God) for the gift of life of our three birds and asked for blessing for a swift and humane kill, giving thanks for all the blessing we receive. Some of the kids didn't like to see it. They were welcome to stay in the classroom, but I thought it was time that they thought of chickens as more than that pale, cold lump of meat on a Styrofoam tray that you buy in a supermarket.

I borrowed an orange traffic cone from the school and turned it upside down, put each chicken into the upside down cone to keep it from flapping its wings and struggling. I cut the bottom of the cone a little larger so the chickens head was sticking out the hole on the bottom. I learned about this from a friend. It's a humane way to kill them because they can't flap around. Then I plucked a few feathers close to the jugular veins near the head to clear a path for the knife and I cut off their heads,

We killed and de-feathered all three chickens. We dry plucked them to save their beautiful feathers for making some feather leis and other feather art. We put the feathers into plastic trash bags and they went into the school freezer to kill any bugs or lice. Then we took the chickens inside to our classroom sink and did a dissection. We opened up the chickens and I showed the students the lungs, heart, liver and intestines. I explained the bile bag or gall bladder and its use for digesting and breaking down the food. We also took out the gizzards, split then in half and I showed them the pebbles and little rocks the chickens eat to help grind up their food since they have no teeth.

The biology teacher heard about it and asked me in to give a talk to his class. He thought it was a great lesson, and he wanted me to leave one of the chickens. The thing is, what he does is he puts everything in a bottle of formaldehyde or whatever and then the students can study it. To me, I feel bad for the bird that has to give up his life just for others to be looking at him. I thought I could do a better service to the chicken, so I didn't give it to the biology teacher. Instead, when we were done with the biology class we went on to Lesson #3: Cooking. I fired up my grill and fed 80 students lunch.

I cut up the chicken into various parts, breast, thighs, wings, drumsticks. Then with a cleaver, I cut those pieces into 1/2 inch pieces and threw everything into a five gallon pot along with ginger, garlic, papaya, green onions and *kalamungay* from our garden. I added some green papayas from our outside garden just to soften it up, because it was tough meat from being out on the road. We had some tomatoes and some Japanese squash from the school garden. I cooked up some rice right there in my classroom, and got more rice from the cafeteria, too. The chicken was little tough, but it tasted good and everybody was happy. Many of our students come from families living in hard conditions, so it made a nice meal for them.

I went home that night feeling a sense of accomplishment, but the next morning I found out that there was a fourth lesson and I was the one who would be learning it. It turns out that some people don't like to hear roosters crowing, and some people don't like to hear them being killed, either. One of the new *haole* teachers complained to the State Department of Health that the chickens were screaming when they were killed. It seemed like normal chicken sounds to me and I don't recall any screaming, but I have a different background I guess. So I ended up getting called up to the principal's office for a chewing out. (Still, I count myself lucky because they never found out about when we slaughtered the cow, the pigs and the deer!)

I did manage to use the chickens to teach my three lessons, with the drawing class, the biology lesson and the sharing of food. I guess Lesson #4 was one that I learned myself, kind of a sad one for me. Rural Maui ways are going away, and being replaced by mainland values: no chickens, no noise. I guess the day will come when there are no more chickens loose out on the roads, just more and more cars and traffic. Much of what I learned from living with my great grandparents was pretty much common sense in the old days. Today, however, these forgotten survival skills of yesterday have become pretty much "uncommon sense!"

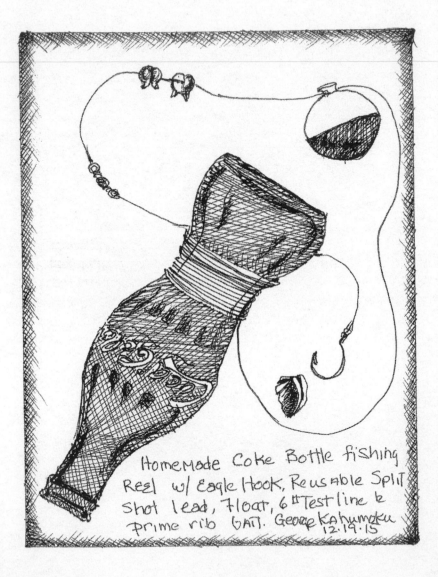

Homemade Coke Bottle fishing
Reel w/ Eagle Hook, Reusable Split
Shot lead, Float, 6# Test line &
Prime rib BAIT. George Kahumoku
12·19·15

# Fishing, Hawaiian Style

My father was a fisherman, as were lots of my family members. We all fished at one time or other, mostly for subsistence and sometimes as a way to make a living. I've loved to go fishing since I was a kid. Of course living on a Pacific island, most of my fishing has been in the ocean and usually on shallow reefs. The thing about fishing is that sometimes you come home with a nice dinner and sometimes you get nothing. But like anything else in life, you don't get anything if you don't try.

In 1999, I went on a music tour to promote my Hymns of Hawai'i album. We stopped in cities along the West coast and one of those stops was in Corvalis, Oregon. We were playing a gig at a restaurant called the Fox & Firkin. There is a road that runs in front of the restaurant and on the other side of the road is a steep slope that leads down to the Willamette River.

We got to the place early, and after I'd finished with the 5 minutes of sound check that I usually need I had a bunch of time on my hands before the show. I asked the folks at the restaurant if there were any fish in the river. The chef told me that occasionally somebody caught a catfish, but there was not much chance of that. "I love catfish!" I told the chef. He smiled at me and said, "You catch one, I'll cook it for you."

I went back outside and looked out at the river. It would be tough to get down that slope. And of course, I had no fishing license and no fishing gear. Still, I had to try. I went down the street a ways and found a Ben Franklin store that sold fishing hooks, line and other stuff. I got what I needed, including a one day license, and headed back to the restaurant for some bait. I figured that a hunk of beef liver would be just the thing for catfish. They didn't have any liver, so what they gave me was a piece of raw, sliced prime rib. They also provided me with a couple of glass coke bottles that we could use as cheap fishing reels for winding up the line.

We were traveling that leg of the trip with my friend Wendy and her 8 year old son, Ben. He and I had kind of bonded, and he followed me everywhere. He was excited about the idea of catching a fish, but got discouraged when they told us that we wouldn't catch anything. I really didn't think we would either, but I told Ben that we should at least try.

Ben and I took our fishing gear and scrambled down the slope to the edge of the river. It was flowing fast. I saw an eddy in the river that I figured would be a great place to hang out if I were a fish. I showed Ben how to wind the line around the bottle and secure it.

What you do is you tie your line to the narrow waist of the coke bottle and secure it real good. Then you wind on at least 50 to 100 yards of 6-15 pound test line. In this case we used 6 pound test line from the Ben Franklin store. Then we tied a piece of lead on the other end of the line about 1/4 size of my thumb and about 18 inches above that lead sinker we tied a loop knot and then added a hook on another looped line that we looped back onto the first loop on the main line. Then we put a floater about 3 feet above the sinker.

Ben and I each made a homemade coke bottle reel with a float, hook, and about 50 yards of line with a lead sinker on the end. We each baited our hooks with prime rib and twirled our fishing contraptions in the air above our heads making sure we didn't hook on to any trees or branches. We each cast and hurled our lines out into that ebb we saw in the Willamette River. After we cast our lines out, we did what all fishermen do. We waited.

Before long it was time for my gig, so I went back up the hill. Ben stayed at the top by the road to keep an eye on the lines. A couple of hours later I was getting ready to do the last song when Ben burst into the place. "Uncle, Uncle! We caught something!" So that was the end of the gig. I put my guitar down and ran outside and worked my way down the slope. Sure enough, one of the floats was completely submerged and we had a fish on the line. Ben reeled the fish close to shore but he didn't know how to land it without a net. I took the line from Ben and gave the line a pull and a jerk and in a moment we had our catch flopping on the river bank.

To our surprise, instead of a catfish we had a beautiful seven pound steelhead trout. I carried it up the slope to the restaurant and gave it to the chef. It turned out that he really didn't have any idea how to clean a fish. He never expected us to catch one! So I ended up doing it myself. I prepared it Hawaiian style, meaning with whatever I had available. In a commercial restaurant, I had everything I wanted. I made a stuffing with crab and shrimp, seasoned with sausage, crab, ginger and finely chopped green onions. We wrapped the fish in foil and cooked it on the grill. When it was done, we shared it with our whole tour crew and Ben got to eat the first fish he'd ever caught.

The chef never really expected me to catch anything, but as I've always believed, you won't get anything unless you try.

George Kahumoku, Jr.

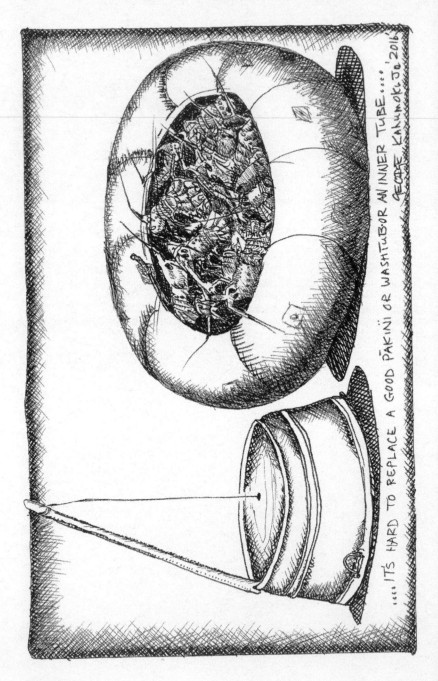

"....IT'S HARD TO REPLACE A GOOD PĀKINI OR WASHTUB-OR AN INNER TUBE...." GEORGE KAHUMOKU JR. 2016

94

# Taking Back the Beach

In 1974, I returned to Hawai'i after graduation from college on the mainland. I was only 23 years old, but I was about to play a role in opening up Hawaiian shores for indigenous people as well as for all of Hawai'i *nei*. It was not something I intended to do, but I kind of fell into it.

I had gotten my degree from the California College of Arts and Crafts in Oakland. Some of my classes were held at U.C. Berkeley. That part of the country, and especially that university, was alive with protests over human rights in one form or other. I guess that as an indigenous person myself, I had a lot of sympathy for oppressed minorities. In Berkeley I learned a lot about peaceful protests, and about using the legal system to support an important cause. On Telegraph Avenue there were protests about the war in Viet Nam. I remember protests at People's Park. There were boycotts headed by Caesar Chavez against big corporations like Safeway. They were aimed at improving working conditions for the United Farm Workers, which included many Mexicans and third world people like me. I even participated in the Third World Arts Festival at the San Francisco Museum of Art, and I went door to door handing out leaflets to get a young black man named Ron Dellums elected into office in Alameda County. I was also part of a non-profit group called the Artist Resource Center. The goal was to keep the arts in the public schools and show the work of up-and-coming artists like me, along with mainstream art. I also helped launch an alternative school using the arts to reach at-risk kids in Oakland. In a nut shell, I learned about community organizing and how important it was to get involved in one's community.

As it turned out, it wasn't long before I used what I had learned to help win important rights for my fellow Hawaiians, as well as for all people who visit the islands.

For generations in Hawai'i, there was no such thing as private land ownership. Generations of families farmed and lived on the same land, but there were no formal deeds — they were not necessary. They lived under a *konahiki* (chief) system and were free to live, fish and hunt in the *ahu pua'a* where they chose to live. Farmers upslope or *mauka* would provide fruits and vegetables, and fishermen at the shore on the *makai* side caught fish. We traded among family and friends. I grew up knowing these old, traditional ways. Even after foreign settlers arrived from the mainland and claimed land, there was still an unwritten tradition of allowing passage by Hawaiian people so they could

96

access important fishing spots and religious areas.

I have always loved to farm, but my father and grandfathers were also fishermen and I've fished all my life. Once I began my music career at the Mauna Kea Beach Hotel on the Big Island, fishing became more of a hobby for me. But whenever I learned about a good run of fish, I was glad to get back on the water.

On the last day of August, 1974, I was gearing up for the start of lobster season the following day. I was going to go to Kaunaoa Bay, located in South Kohala. There was a great fishing spot to the left of the Mauna Kea Beach Hotel, which was owned by the Rockefeller family from New York. I had wonderful memories of a day when I was 11 or 12. I was with my dad and my cousins and we got a nice catch of lobsters. We roasted them on an open fire and topped them with lemon butter, and soy sauce with chili pepper water. We dipped them in sweet sour sauce with ginger. Delicious!

With this memory in mind, I started my preparations for lobster season. From my cousin Kikino Navarro, who worked at Mauna Kea Sugar, I had acquired an old, patched-up big-truck inner tube. It was the perfect size for my *pakini* (galvanized wash tub) that was also used to play wash tub base. The *pakini* fit perfectly into the *puka* or donut hole of the inner tube. With a bit of nylon rope I made some knotted netting to go around the tube, which could be towed in the water. The tub fit down perfectly inside and now I had a nice Hawaiian-style floating container to hold my catch of lobster.

On a warm evening on August 31, I parked my truck on the hillside above the Mauna Kea Hotel beach, about 1/4 mile above the bay. My preparation was working perfectly. It was easy to roll the inner tube down the old trail and right into the water. I just had to be careful to avoid the *kiawe* (mesquite) thorns so it wouldn't puncture my inner tube. Lobster season didn't start until after midnight, but I was using an old Hawaiian trick I learned from my uncle Walter Paulo. You want to be the first to hit the lobster, but you still have to be legal. What you do is make sure that you don't come out of the water with your catch until September 1.

So at around 11 P.M. I hit the water towing my *pakini*, and wearing my mask, fins and snorkel. I had an underwater flashlight, and I set about looking for lobsters. I hoped that I might get 4 or 5 of them, but as the night went on I kept finding more. By 5 A.M. I had 22 of them! I swam to the beach towing my pakini full of spiny lobster. As I pulled my catch onto the sand I realized that I had a problem. It had been easy to roll the *pakini* in the inner tube down to the beach, but getting it back up the hill 1/4 mile to my truck was going to be pretty hard with it full of 22 live spiny lobsters.

That's when I saw a couple of big Hawaiian guys in hotel shirts and slacks walking towards me. I was glad to see them. I had so many lobsters, I knew that I would be sharing them with lots of others. If these big fellows would be willing to give me a hand getting my catch to the truck, I would be happy to give them all the lobsters they wanted. Heck, we could share in the ocean's bounty with seven lobsters each, divided among the three of us. We'd even have one extra to share with someone else. That's the Hawaiian way I had learned from my *kupuna* (elders) and my ancestors!

As the guys got closer, I noticed that they had something shiny reflecting from their shirts from the rising morning sun. Then I noticed they were wearing uniforms and that the shiny reflections were badges that they wore on their chests. I soon found out, that they weren't there to help. They asked me what my name was and I said, "George Kahumoku Jr." Then one of them put his hand on my shoulder and said, "George Kahumoku Jr., you are under arrest for trespassing on private land." They said that the beach in front of the Mauna Kea Beach Hotel was private and I had no right to my catch.

The police were called and instead of going home with a wonderful treat for family and friends, I ended up in handcuffs in the back of a police car. I was taken to the Waimea police station and booked for trespassing on private property. It was the third time I'd been arrested. The first was when I was surfing in Waikiki too close to the Waikiki Wall and get arrested with my friend and classmate Wayne Wong. The second was when I was collared during a protest rally at the People's Park in Berkeley. I wasn't involved in the protest, I was just standing there watching, but I got hauled away anyway.

I spent a few hours sitting in a cell in the Waimea jail in a wet bathing suit. I have to say that I was pretty mad about what had just happened. From small kid time, I was so used to the idea that we Hawaiians had a right to gather fish from our ocean. Getting arrested for fishing just didn't feel fair or right to me. Eventually my uncle Pila came down and bailed me out. It had been a disappointing day, to say the least. I didn't mind so much losing the lobster, but it's hard to find a *pakini* that could double as a bass and also be used as a container to hold lobster or fish. It was even harder to find a used plantation truck tire inner tube to use as a float for the works.

I guess this might have been the end of the story if I hadn't had my Berkeley college experience. The next day I got to wondering if other Hawaiians had also been arrested. One thing I'd learned in college was the importance of protesting people to stick together. You get one guy willing to fight back, then the next and the next and pretty soon you have an army! So instead of just taking it lying down, I went off to Hilo to have a look at court records. I had heard locals talk about being denied access to traditional fishing spots and I wanted to find how many of these arrests were taking place. What I got was a big surprise. There were hundreds of arrests! I thought that it was very wrong, and that if we Hawaiians get together, we might be able to force a change in the law.

I had a bunch of names from court cases and I starting talking to people. It turned out that the *kupuna* had been unhappy about this for years, but they didn't have the energy or knowhow to fight. They needed young blood. They needed me, and many others like me, willing to join together. We began to have public meetings at a local elementary school, and one of the people there suggested contacting the Hawai'i Legal Aid Society. A small delegation of us made an appointment and went to their office in Hilo.

The Legal Aid Society was in a storefront in a run-down building in downtown Hilo. There were two lawyers there, and they did not inspire a lot of confidence. The senior guy was Ben Gaddis, and he was quite young. He had red hair in an afro, wore Mod Squad glasses, and he spoke with a Southern accent. To me, he seemed like a refugee from the sixties. He was dressed in a frilled shirt, black and white shoes, and a plaid sports jacket. He had on green bell-bottom pants. He looked like kind of a polyester leprechaun. The other guy, Andy Levin, looked like a lawyer from New York. He was, in fact, a lawyer from New York. He was wearing a tie and an actual dark blue suit, with the pants nearly matching the coat. He was also just out of law school.

After hearing why we were there, Ben and Andy explained to us that they usually handled divorces and other domestic matters, restraining orders, etc. We knew that many times these guys were representing people who couldn't pay cash and instead paid them with pigs or chickens. But they were a couple of good guys and when they learned how many folks were behind us, they said that they would look into the matter. I think they really felt the momentum of our movement. All they asked of us was to stay interested, stay organized, and show up in court when necessary. We had a list of phone numbers, and we continued our meetings at the Keaukaha elementary school. Ben had told us that we would have to be patient. He was right. It was two years until we had our first day in court.

The Hilo courthouse is in the harbor area. It was one of the few buildings in that part of Hilo that did not get destroyed in the 1946 tsunami. The many buildings that had existed next to the courthouse were never rebuilt, and there were just vacant lots full of weeds there. In September of 1974, those lots were packed with cars. The courtroom was overflowing. Ben said to show up, and we did, in the hundreds!

At our table were our two lawyers, Ben and Andy in their usual outfits. At the other table were the attorneys representing the Rockefellers, who owned the Mauna Kea Beach Hotel. There were ten of them, all dressed alike. Their dark suits were made of some kind of material that glimmered and changed colors as they moved around. Their pants matched their coats and they all had red neckties. Compared to them, our guys looked like Bozo the clown and his skinny sidekick. Seeing the opposition compared to our lawyers, we thought that we were going to lose. But Ben and Andy were good, and they knew their stuff. It also turned out that we had gotten the right judge, a guy named Ernest Kubota. He was a young Japanese Judge who was *hanaied* (adopted) by a Hawaiian Family in

Papaikou and he had fished for lobster in Kaunaoa Bay where we were all arrested.

I wish I could say that we won our case that day, but nothing got resolved that first day in court, and not in the many more court days over the next several years. But Ben and Andy were true to the Hawaiian people and they stayed in there fighting even when Andy went into private practice. Finally, in 1982, almost ten years later, the Supreme Court of the State of Hawai'i ruled in our favor. From that time on, the principle was established that all beaches in all the islands are public property up to the high tide line. Mauna Kea properties ended up having to give public access by providing 45 parking stalls in their parking lot with access to the beach! They also provided showers and toilets and a paved access trail down to the beach. In fact, because of this court case, every single beach in the entire state of Hawai'i has public access with parking as well as showers provided. My role in this case was a small one, but I am proud to have been a part of the hundreds of people who came forward to get public access to the beaches in the State of Hawai'i for all to enjoy!

Ben Gaddis got a new suit and eventually became a Judge in Hilo. Both he and Andy Levin continued to work with Legal Aid throughout their careers. They are now retired and still live on the Big Island.

# Teaching for Life

I 've always been a teacher, and I've loved it. But I've learned over the years that even though you try your very best, you can't reach every kid. You take great pride and satisfaction in the ones you can help, and there is often disappointment in others. I think that these differences are even larger when you're dealing with what we often call "at risk" kids. That's been my specialty since the beginning of my career.

I don't know, maybe everybody is "at risk" in life. We all start out with some set of values that guides us and determines what kind of person we'll turn out to be. I could have gone either way. Plenty of people close to me from both my family and from students I have taught have been in jail. From my experiences, good and bad, as a student at Kamehameha Schools, from my mom and dad, from my *kupuna* (elders), and from my many mentors and teachers, I learned what good teaching is and saw how it can impact a kid's life. But for me the point is that everyone deserves a chance, and I don't see my "at risk" students as just a bunch of bad kids.

I suppose you could say that my career has followed a different path from most teachers. I grew up in the old Hawaiian ways. Even though I have a master's degree in education, I am most comfortable speaking my native pidgin. And while I certainly learned a lot in formal classrooms at Kamehameha and going to college in California, I think that my real depth of knowledge and common sense comes from being raised mostly by grandparents. Their generation spans back to years when we Hawaiians were mostly self-sufficient and had to depend on our own selves for survival. From them I learned to develop hands-on skills through observation, looking at options for decision making and problem solving, and just plain thinking about surviving and making a living.

When I began teaching in Hawai'i, it was with kids who had a similar background to mine, but maybe mostly didn't have all the advantages that I had in terms of the values of honesty and hard work that were instilled into me. I guess it was natural that I would end up wanting to teach kids who were kind of on the edge of getting into trouble and leading marginal lives. I thought that maybe I was in a good position, as a Hawaiian man, to help them find themselves. That's how I ended up teaching "Special Motivation" kids at Lahainaluna High School. To get into my class you had to cut classes more than 23 out of 44 days for two quarters in a row. And, you had to get an "F" grade in 6 of your 7 classes. My classroom was in an area of school grounds separated from the rest of Lahainaluna High School at the end of the dirt parking lot. I sometimes thought that maybe the rest of the school liked to keep these kids separate because they were the troublemakers.

I was one of the few Hawaiian teachers at Lahainaluna, and a lot of the kids would see me and start out thinking that they can just slide by. I'm Hawaiian, they're Hawaiian. But they quickly learned that the exact opposite is how it will be with me. My students do learn a lot of things that you wouldn't usually get in school. We did school work, of course. Thanks to my music connections we had more computers than any other classroom in school, because I thought it was important that the kids learn about these things. But we also did gardening, and grew and shared all kinds of great food. They learned all about irrigation and fertilization, in addition to school stuff. We composed poetry, stories and songs, and played and shared music.

My grandparents were observers of nature and I guess I got that from them. I could sit and watch a fish tank for hours. In the same way, even though I'm talking and teaching, I'm always observing the kids. For me as a teacher, I look at a kid and I figure that they're going to be living a long time, so what can I do in this small amount of time we have together? Really, I'm just a very small slice of their life so I try to be as compassionate as I can and to be real. But I'm realistic. There are plenty that I cannot help.

They probably belong in jail, not in school but I give them the benefit of the doubt at the moment. What I always try to do when I work with any kind of kid, is find their strengths. We all know what their weaknesses are. That's why they're in my "special motivation" class. I try to get their attention and let them develop their strengths and build on that. Then we shore up the weaknesses and build self-esteem so they have confidence. Once you get that going, hopefully the rest will kick in. So I've used music, creative arts, gardening, food prep and peer pressure to motivate my kids to success.

Later, I get to see the kids I taught at Lahainaluna in the community, and I see that they're leading really wonderful lives. Not all of them, of course. If you've been to Maui and parked your rental car in a remote area, only to return and find your window busted and your stuff missing, there's a good chance that it was one of my students. I went to visit my brother in Sagauro Correctional Facility in Arizona a few years back. Walking down an alley-way of cells I got to see maybe a half dozen of my students from Lahainaluna. They recognized me. "Hey Mistah! Hey Mistah! Kahumokes! If we would have listened to you we wouldn't be here today." I'm just saying that I've seen both ends of the spectrum.

One of my most painful teaching experiences was with a young girl, a high school senior. She had been in a lot of trouble in the past for drugs. I saw real potential in her and I devoted a lot of time and attention to her. She really seemed to be turning the corner. On her 18th birthday, I brought a cake to school for her, something I've never done for a student before. I had the cake in the fridge, ready to surprise her at lunch time. Then I got the surprise. A couple of Lahaina cops showed up. They had found drugs in her locker. Usually they would have cited her and referred her to family court. But because she was 18 that day, she was treated as an adult and was taken out of the classroom in handcuffs. That incident was probably the most disappointing of my teaching career, and the unhappy memory stayed with me for a long time. But ten years later I ran into her again and I was glad to see that she had turned her life around and was doing well. She was working for a major airline as a booking agent and had started a family! You never know.

When I teach a person in my classroom sometimes I'm not going to remember their names, because I've taught thousands of kids. But I think my relationship with them is not only that moment or that semester or that school year but really for life. So when I teach them I expect our relationship to continue until the end of our lives. And I have had that same relationship with a lot of my teachers. I've kept in touch with many of them over the years.

Some of my students got arrested for growing *pakalolo* (marijuana) on the slopes of West Maui. They had learned what I had taught them about farming, fertilization and irrigation, and their plants were thriving. The only problem was, their plants were doing so well that when the season turned dry, their plots stood out brilliant green on the brown slopes and the cops knew exactly where to find them. It's the triumph and the tears of teaching. They paid attention in school and learned what I taught them. Then they got themselves in trouble by putting my good lessons to bad use.

That's teaching, the good and the bad.

A Hawaiian Life Volume 2

# George and the Magic Seeds

There's this old joke about a reporter for a small-town newspaper who is writing a question-of-the-week feature. He goes around asking people what they would do if they won a million dollars in the lottery. After talking to people around town, the reporter goes out into the countryside where he spots a farmer working on his tractor in a big field. When he is asked about the million dollars the farmer thinks about it for a moment, then he says, "Well I reckon I'd just keep on farming until it was all gone."

For me, this is not really much of a joke. In Hawai'i we used to have what they now call a sustainable economy. We are the people of the canoe, and we brought all the stuff we needed to be sustainable with us to survive in Hawai'i. We brought hundreds of varieties of taro, sweet potatoes, tapioca, bananas, kukui nut trees, breadfruit, yams, sugar cane, *awa*: the list goes on and on. We had a diversity of plants, and hundreds of varieties of food and herbs to sustain ourselves. The Hawaiian Islands are the most remote occupied islands in the world, and we had no choice. If we didn't take care of ourselves we would starve to death. I was brought up in the old ways and learning to fish and farm was taught to me early. But I love to farm so much that it's almost an addiction, and I keep on farming even though at times I've lost a lot of money doing it. Farming is a risky business, but maybe it appeals to me because I'm a risk-taker.

Back in 1975 I had a good job on the Big Island as director of *Alu Like*, a non-profit organization for native Hawaiians. After a while I think they were getting a little tired of dealing with me. I have always been kind of a free spirit, and I didn't fit so well with their organization. To me, it seemed like they'd rather push paper than get things done.

One of the things I really felt strongly about was getting hold of some land located in Kohala. We could farm it and raise plenty of crops to feed ourselves. When I couldn't get *Alu Like* to go along with me on the project, I started trying to organize the local community to go after the land. I had a lot of community support for this project. When *Alu Like* wouldn't work with me on this I quit the job. They were probably happy to see me go, but my family wasn't too pleased with my rashness.

Eventually I ended up farming that land by myself. Really, it was more like I was gardening at the time, but on a pretty big scale. While living in Hilo, I had a huge garden with taro, sweet Potato, bananas, *ho'i'o* or *pohole* (fern shoots), *ulu* (bread fruit) and things growing all over. I had about eleven acres of wild fruits, bananas, breadfruit. It had been a jungle that was partially cleared and planted with bananas and taro already, behind the gulch next to the Chinese Grave yard where I lived in Hilo on Ululani Street. I wasn't doing anything commercial, just feeding our family.

I told my *ohana* (family) that I wanted to raise crops commercially. They were pretty skeptical, but they gave me a budget of $200 to go try to do my farming thing. I joined the Puna Young Farmers organization and made new friends there. There was a couple there named Rusty and Jenny. Jenny told me to go see this guy named Henry Suzuki. He had a limp from shrapnel in his leg and one of his hands was deformed from a grenade or something that went off in his hand. He had been a member of the 442nd Regimental Combat team of the 100th Infantry Battalion. These were the Japanese American soldiers who fought in Europe. They were known as the "Purple Heart Battalion" because they took so many losses due to their bravery in combat. They were the most decorated infantry regiment in the history of the U.S. army, with 21 Medal of Honor awards. I told Henry I wanted to farm. He said "Okay," and wrote something in Japanese on this piece of paper. I didn't know what the heck it said, but when he asked me to, I signed it. He sent me to go see this other guy at Hilo Farmer's Exchange.

115

The Hilo Farmers Exchange is not what it sounds like. It's just this weird little store in downtown Hilo, where they sell all kinds of stuff, including old military gear as well as tools, plants and fertilizer.

I went there and asked for the guy I was supposed to see. This man looked at the paper, looked at me, and said, "Henry Suzuki sent you?"

I nodded. I didn't know it at the time but this guy was another member of the 442nd. He gave me another close look and finally said, "Okay." He went into a back room and I could hear him rummaging around looking for something. After a while the searching got more frantic, and he started yelling at his wife for moving his stuff. Finally, he reappeared with a little zip-lock bag with handwritten Japanese writing on it. It was full of tiny seeds. He carefully measured out some of them in a teaspoon, weighed them, and put them into this little manila envelope, one of those small 1" X 3" things. He carefully licked it, put tape over the whole thing, and put it cautiously in my hand. I felt like he had given me magic seeds, although I didn't know what kind of seed they were.

"Now, treasure this," he said to me. "Be careful with this seed." Then he wrote something on a piece of paper and handed it to me. It was a bill for $120! For a couple of teaspoons of seed! Wow! I was blown away! This was already a big part of my farming budget. So what did I do? I paid him, of course. Talk about blind faith. But that's me.

116

I went home that afternoon and told my *ohana*, "Oh, look what I got, I got these seeds. They cost $120." My *tutu* (grandmother) asked what kind of seeds they were and I said, "I don't know."

"What!" she yelled. "You mean you paid a hundred and twenty bucks for some kind of seeds and you don't know what they are?!" She was so mad she tore the envelope open and flung the seeds all over the house. She was so angry at me for being so gullible, listening to these two Japanese guys. The thing is, I really didn't know what kind of seed I had. My *tutu* stormed out of the house, and as soon as she was gone I was down on my knees going around the house picking up all the seeds one by one. They were in the carpet, on the furniture, all over the place. I don't know how many seeds I got, but I think I got most of them.

So I went back to Henry and he told me I should go and talk to Jenny at the Puna Farmers. I showed her the seeds and she was pretty surprised. "Henry gave you these? He must really like you." She explained to me that Henry and the other members of the 442nd were a very close-knit group who were bound for life. Once Henry accepted me, I was in the inner circle. She told me about my seeds. They were a very rare hybrid variety of Japanese cucumber. She told me the best way to plant the seeds, and advised me to use trellises if I really wanted to get good results. I didn't have money to buy trellises, so I went up to Mountain View on the side of the volcano and cut some strawberry guava sticks to use as trellis posts.

I wasn't sure about how to set them up, so I ended up going back to Henry. He sent me to another 442nd veteran who sells netting for trellises. I bought 40 rolls of netting, each 7 feet high and 100 feet long, and installed it on the guava posts. And that was the end of my $200 budget. I prayed that this was going to work.

Within a few days, I had some beautiful cucumber seedlings. A couple of days after that, half of them were gone. I didn't know what the heck to do. I called Jenny and told her what happened. She told me that the problem was cutworm, and I have to spray with an insecticide. I had used up half the seeds, and now I had to use up all the rest. But the insecticide worked and the vines started to flourish.

I was watering by hand at first. But then I spoke with Henry and he said "No, no, brah, you have to put in irrigation or you're not going to be able to keep up with watering them." He wrote me another note in Japanese and sent me to this guy named Roy Kimura. Kimura was another veteran, and he was missing an arm. "Henry sent you?" he asked. I said, "Yes." He then grabbed a piece of paper and a long 300 foot measuring tape. He dropped everything he was doing and told his workers he was going with me! "Let's go," he said and we jumped in my truck and traveled 7 miles out to our farm in Paukaa to take a look.

He made a quick sketch and we taped and measured everything. It took us almost 4 hours, and finally I took him back to his shop. He told me to come back in two days.

When I returned, he had made a drawing and he had laid out all the equipment I would need, all the irrigation hoses, in-line pressure regulators, PVC pipes and fittings with valves, everything, and he told me the cost would be two thousand dollars.

I thought to myself, *Wow! Two thousand dollars! I can't afford that!* But he said, "Don't Worry Henry says you're good for it. So I put in two thousand dollars worth of irrigation with a main and eight sub-main open and close valves. "You cannot afford the automatic system, so you'll have to go and turn and switch on and off the various the valves every 6 hours," Roy told me. It was pretty complicated, like every six hours turn on this valve, turn off that valve and so on, so I can water different sections at a time. He even measured the pressure of the water coming in. So I did all that and when the plants were about 4 weeks old they were 18 inches high, just climbing up the trellis.

All around me where I was farming, it was all cane land. My farm was in the middle of a cane field in the back yard of this guy named Doc Adler. Doc also had a swimming pool in his yard. He was very good about letting me use his property for access, going through his gate, over a little bridge and around his pool. I kept him in cucumbers and cabbage. It's kind of a variation on the old Hawaiian ways.

Things seemed to be going along pretty well and I was hopeful of a good crop. That's when hurricane Eva hit. Eva was one of the worst storms to ever strike Hawai'i. It did a huge amount of damage everywhere. Because my field was surrounded by ten to twelve foot high cane, the cucumbers were pretty well sheltered from the wind for most of the storm. Eventually, though, the cane was flattened. I was kind of afraid to look at the damage, I have to tell you. But when I went to check on the farm a couple of days after the storm, I found the cucumbers growing like crazy.

With the extra water from Eva, and with the sun not blocked by the cane, the crop just took off. Not only that, but it seemed that I had about the only cucumber field left in the whole state of Hawai'i. The price of cucumbers took off. Usually cucumbers go for about 25 cents a pound for grade one, grade two's for 15 cents and off-grade is five cents a pound. After the storm it was a dollar fifty for grade ones, grade twos were a dollar and off-grade went for 75 cents each. So literally, every cucumber I was picking was a buck, two bucks. In less than six weeks I made almost $42,000 off this one cucumber patch. And I was picking twice a day. It was like harvesting water. In the morning, I would see cucumbers about two three inches long and by afternoon they would be seven or eight inches. If they're over a foot long it's all off-grade, but even off- grades were making more money because they use off-grade in the hotels. I was making money hand over foot. I know it sounds like I was off to a great start as a farmer but really it was the beginning of the end.

As soon as I had some money, I planted a couple of acres of ginger. On those acres I made over $300,000. I just kept on going from there. The next year I planted a couple more acres. At one point I had almost 25 acres of ginger. Most small farmers had only around 5 acres each. I had more ginger than Hawai'i could use and I needed to find bigger markets. I had gone to school in Oakland California with a guy whose parents owned some produce stores. And from the one connection in Oakland, I got another connection in Canada, then New Orleans, New York City, and even France, Germany and England. I found out that the Chinese communities are very much connected all over the world. I was sending ginger to wherever there's a Chinatown. I was sending up container loads. Every week I'd send one container load which is 25,000 pounds of Chinese root ginger.

Supply and demand for crops can be pretty hard to predict. Just when things seemed to be going great, the bottom dropped out of the ginger market. Chinese root ginger was coming in from Fiji and the price dropped from $1.25 a pound to $.26 a pound! Yes!

I was getting 26 cents a pound, but my cost was around 30 cents a pound. I should have stopped, but I was stubborn and I thought the market would come back. Instead, it kept going down. Before long I was about $90,000 in the hole and I had to walk away from the farm. I went back to teaching again, and in a couple years I worked myself out of debt. Since then, I've ranched and farmed over 3000 acres in

North Kohala growing alfalfa hay and raising cattle. Over the past 40 years, I've also raised and marketed pigs, guavas, taro, coffee, avocados, macnuts and *ti* leaf from my South Kona Kealia Farms. Today, I continue to grow taro and now market our Hawaiian herbal teas, coffee, bananas, papaya, lilikoi and other fresh farm fruits and vegetables, goats, sheep, honey and mixed greens to Local Harvest- our organic marketing co-op here on Maui.

At times, I have felt as if my music and teaching just serve to support my farming habit. The thing is, I love being on the land and growing things. It's a big part of my Hawaiian soul. Even weeding is a favorite thing that calms me and gives me focus. For native planters like me, weeding is meditation.

I still love to farm, though now I just grow crops for my family and friends. I'm still trying everyday to balance the books and my life thorough being sustainable and farming, playing music and mentoring the next generation.

THE POWER OF LA'AU KAHEA.

LA'AU KAHEA: I called out: Tree, CHAINSAW, PLEASE FORGIVE MY COUSIN WALTER... HE NEEDS TO LIVE TO HELP RAISE HIS FAMILY ...2016. George Kahumoku Jr.

# The Power of La'au Kahea

L a'au kahea is a practice of traditional Hawaiian medicine. It is a way to promote healing with prayers and chants. It is usually used in combination with native island herbs. Many people don't believe in this sort of thing and I can understand that. For others there is a fascination with the mysticism and magic from the culture of Hawai'i. You may or may not be a believer, but for me. I've had a lot of personal experience with this kind of thing and its part of who I am as a Hawaiian man. La'au kahea literally saved my life, as well as the life of a friend when we were working chainsaws! But first, you should know how this all came to pass.

Back in the mid 70's, I headed an alternative school called Hale O Ho'oponopono, located at Honaunau, down at the City of Refuge on the big island. It was there that I met several kupuna (elders). Some of them were also kahuna, kind of a Hawaiian shaman. Through them I began feeling connected with my ancestors and the spirit world, as well as learning practical applications for healing the mind and body.

For many of us, the 70's were a time of re-discovery of being a native Hawaiian. It was a kind of Hawaiian Renaissance. Eddie and Myrna Kamae and the Sons of Hawai'i, and Dennis Kamakahi were researching and creating both new and old songs. The Hokule'a sailing canoe was preparing to rediscover navigation through the stars and currents. In Congress, native Hawaiians were being recognized as native Americans. Merrie Monarch was reviving the lost arts of hula, and chants and Hawaiian culture was on everyone's mind. Several members of The Protect Kaho'olawe *Ohana* were arrested for occupying and trying to get back the island of Kahoolawe. John Irangihau, from our Maori cousins in New Zealand, planted the seed of *punana leo* (Hawaiian language schools) and the teaching and relearning of our Hawaiian language. My brother Moses and I were in the thick of it and by the late 70's, we recorded the now legendary *"Hi'ipoi I ka Aina Aloha"* with Aunty Edith Kanaka'ole. I played slack key guitar and Moses played bass.

We were relearning and redefining our connection to each other and our Hawaiian culture. This was stuff that we never learned in college or at Kamehameha Schools. We would sleep on our *heiaus* (sacred places) so we could feel the spirits. Then we were taught to distinguish between a male and a female spirit. When we got chicken-skin on the left side of our body, we were taught that this was a *wahine* (woman) spirit we were dealing with. If we got

126

chicken-skin on the right side of our body, we were taught that we were feeling a male spirit. We lay on the trails face down so we could feel and hear the spirits of the night marchers! We were told that those spirits that walked on our backs softly were our *ohana* or relatives. Anyway, this spirit world was very new and exciting and we were curious.

Eventually I learned a form of healing called *la'au kahea* or calling out of an object, inanimate and animate, from our *kupuna*, Uncle Abraham Moses. His simple theory and advice was that when you stumbled on a rock or branch on a trail, instead of cursing under your breadth, you call out to the branch or rock by calling out and saying "branch" or "rock," you were here first! I'm sorry to have disturbed you, please forgive me." Instant healing takes place and the pain in your foot would go away! Same thing for a sliced finger. Put the knife on the sliced finger and say "Knife, you were here first, please forgive me," and the bleeding would stop and the finger would heal.

Anyway, I was able to use this simple form of healing several times. The most memorable healings I received, however, involved not knives or rocks but chainsaws.

The first time, I was in North Kohala cutting down and trimming branches of a 20-acre Beaumont Guava Orchard with my cousin Michael Naihe. We each had a chainsaw. Michael was very deliberate and mindful in his use of his saw. Being me, I took a different approach more suited to my personality. What I was doing was using my saw like a ninja, slashing and cutting on the upswing as well as the downswing. I thought I was being very efficient. No movement was wasted. I was used to clearing our land of invasive Christmas Berries, Rosy apple, Guava and *hau* and *kukui* brush and trees.

On this day, however, I was a little bit too enthusiastic and over-confident. On this one slash I cut through this 8-inch guava branch on a downswing and my chainsaw just ripped into it! My hands must have been tired from the previous 12 hours of chain sawing because before I could pull that chainsaw back on the upswing, I sawed through that 8 inch guava log and the chainsaw continued cutting through my blue jeans and right through my left upper thigh to my thigh bone. It happened so fast! There was the sound of the chain saw cutting through the log, then the sound of soft flesh being cut. Zzzzzzep! My Flesh! Then there was a splatter of blood, <u>my</u> blood, all over the cut log and chain saw and bushes nearby.

Michael was working in the next row of trees about 50 feet away from me. I gave out a yell and he came a-running. We were up in the mountains 45 minutes from civilization, and I began to bleed. I mean I began to gush and bleed real bad! From my youthful Boy Scout experience, I knew what I had to do. I took out my handkerchief to make a tourniquet but my thigh was too big around and the handkerchief was too short to go around.

Right then and there, in that very instant, I remembered what our Kupuna uncle Abraham

Moses taught us about *la'au kahea*. I placed my cut thigh next to that living cut guava branch and placed my chainsaw on my leg thigh and I called out. "Tree, Guava tree, and Chainsaw, please forgive me! You were here first. We are clearing this land to raise cattle and raise guava for food! Please forgive me!" And you know what? The bleeding stopped in its tracks. I took off my pants and my thigh was a mess! There was a 6 inch long cut right to the bone. And the cut was 2 inches wide going across my left thigh. I thought to myself, hhhmmmm, left leg, *wahine* problems. Get hurt on the right, male or *kane* problems.

I remembered that I had a sewing kit under my truck seat. It was something I used for stitching up our hunting dogs when they occasionally got cut up from the wild boars we hunted, I got out the needle and thread and stitched myself up. I only felt pain on the side of the cut closest to my heart. I had severed the nerves to the other side of the cut so there was no feeling there when the needle went through my skin.

Anyway, I stitched myself up with 5 stitches, each about 1 inch apart. I didn't have any alcohol, but I had gas mixed with chain saw oil, so I poured that gas oil chain saw mixture on the cut. Man, it burned like hell, but I took the pain. I then cut off the left leg of that pair of blue jeans up to the cut on my thigh and covered my cut with a torn piece of my blue jeans and duct tape. I put my cut jeans back on. I was near the end of my row of guava trees and I wanted to finish cutting, so I continued chain sawing for another hour or so until I finished that row. That evening, I went home with Michael, and soaked that cut with Hawaiian salt with water in the bath tub.

The next day I went to Kohala emergency room to have a look by real medical staff! After a two hour wait, they had a look, re-dressed the wound and complemented me on the good stitching job I had done. Then they charged me $200 bucks for the emergency room visit! Wow! One week later, I removed the stitches myself to save money. Today I can still see that scar on my left thigh.

Another memorable time I used *la'au kahea* also involved chain saws. This time, I was in Kealia South Kona, clearing my great grandfather Willy Kahumoku's property about 1/2 mile in an inaccessible area up the mountains off the main road. My cousin Walter Boy Henriques was helping me. He had just gotten out of jail and he had a lot of vented up anger. He was cutting down a thick grove of Christmas berries next to me and he was going at it ninja style. The branches were a tangled mess, intertwined and connected. I warned him about the way he was cutting. From experience! I cut the branches from underneath the canopy and cut the long branches into short 3-6 feet logs. The way the canopy was tangled, it was like cutting a needle in a haystack. Walter was cutting from the top and I could see an accident just waiting to happen. I tried to warn him, but I was too late! Before I could get to him, he cut his last branch that was loaded with the weight of the previous branches he had cut, all connected.

And then bam! The branch snapped back and hit him square in the face! If fact, it hit him in the nose and pushed his nose right into his brain. From my experience with martial arts, I knew that this is a move for destroying and killing one's opponent. Push your opponent's nose into their brain. To me Walter was a dead man! In that instant, I remembered the power of *la'au kahea.*

My cousin was knocked out and he seemed to be comatose. The chain saw was still screaming in his hand! I pulled the choke and flooded his chainsaw to kill the motor. Then I put his head next to the Christmas berry stump he had just cut and I put that warm chain saw blade on his head and I called out, "Tree, Christmas berry tree, and chainsaw, please forgive my cousin Walter and let him live! He has two young boys and a wife to care for. Please help him! With the love of God, please help my cousin survive!" Then it was totally quiet. Even the birds stopped singing. I felt the cool *mauka* (mountain) winds subside, and the warm *nahenahe* (gentle) *makai* (ocean) winds started to blow. And I waited and waited. Forty-five minutes or so went by.

Then I got all chicken-skin, and the chicken-skin travelled to my left side, and I could feel our tutu's love pour into my cousin. And right there and then, I saw my cousin's contorted face heal! His nose popped right back out and he proceeded to awaken from his sleep. When he was fully awake, he was angry again and wanted to keep cutting the Christmas Berry tree! I was so happy that he was alive and could walk himself out, and that I didn't have to carry a 280 pound dead body off of that mountain! I told him, let's just cool it, rest, take the rest of the day off and just go for a swim down at the beach and have some lunch. And that's what we did. We packed up our gear and headed down *makai* (to the ocean) to chill out!

People have different ideas about medicine and healing. I have full respect for Western medicine and doctors. But as a Hawaiian man, I have learned to also respect the power of *la'au kahea* as it was taught to me by my *kupuna*.

# The Meaning of Life by George Kahumoku Jr.

To love
To be loved
To help
To be helped
To mentor
To be mentored
To learn
To teach
To share
To be inspired
To inspire others
To know the difference between right and wrong
To experience joy and happiness with all our
    senses
To experience sorrow
To develop physically, mentally, and spiritually
To contribute
To develop our gifts
To use our gifts to serve others
To communicate and connect with others
To create music, dance and song
To let go
To remember
To forget

To be sorry and seek forgiveness
To be thankful
To become an active member of one's
community
To know God
To put into action God's plan
To learn to follow, as well as lead
To create stories
To develop culture and art
To find a partner in life
To create a home for our shelter and for our
spirits
To experience being a child, a parent, and a
grandparent
To heal
To soar
To fly
To work until we're tired
To play
To rest
To dream and to fulfill our dreams
To forgive
To plant
To weed
To harvest
To eat
To experience warm rain on my face and the
promise of another day tomorrow

# Da Show

Would you like to meet George? Each Wednesday evening he performs his Grammy Award winning Hawaiian musical show at the Napili Kai Beach Resort on Maui. Stop by and say hello, and let him know you've read his book. Then sit back, relax, and enjoy some of Hawai'i's finest music and story-telling.

Info snf tickets at www.slackkeyshow.com.

George's website is at www.kahumoku.com

# Recognition for George's Music

## HAWAI'I MUSIC AWARDS

2006  Hymns of Hawai'i, Volume 2
      (with  Daniel Ho)
2005 Masters of Hawaiian Slack Key Guitar
     Volume 1
2010 Masters of Hawaiian Slack Key Guitar
     Volume 2

## NA HOKU HANOHANO AWARDS

2000 Hymns of Hawaii with Daniel Ho
2006 Hymns of Hawaii, Volume 2
2009 Ki Ho Alu Foundation Legacy Award
2010 Moe Keale "Aloha Is" Award

## GRAMMY AWARDS

2005 Masters of Hawaiian Slack Key Guitar
     Volume 1
2006 Legends of Hawaiian Slack Key Guitar
2007 Treasures of Hawaiian Slack Key Guitar
2008 Spirit of Hawaiian Slack Key Guitar
     (nominated)
2009 Masters of Hawaiian Slack Key Guitar
     Volume 2
2012 Wao Akua - The Forest of the Gods
     (nominated)

51696082R00086

Made in the USA
San Bernardino, CA
30 July 2017